In Contact!

Case Studies from the Long War

Volume I

William G. Robertson
General Editor

Combat Studies Institute Press
Fort Leavenworth, Kansas

Library of Congress Cataloging-in-Publication Data

In contact! : case studies from the long war / by William G. Robertson, general editor.
    p. cm.
    1. Iraq War, 2003---Campaigns--Case studies. 2. Iraq War, 2003---Personal narratives, American. 3. Afghan War, 2001---Campaigns--Case studies. 4. Afghan War, 2001---Personal narratives, American. I. Robertson, William Glenn, 1944- II. Title.

DS79.76.I4618 2006
956.7044'3--dc22

2006037270

ISBN 0-16-077374-1

Foreword

With *In Contact! Case Studies from the Long War, Volume I*, the historians of the Combat Studies Institute (CSI) have produced a historical anthology to support Army schools, to promote general professional development in the field, and to inform the American people about the missions performed by their Army in this "long war."

These case studies include both lethal and nonlethal missions performed by Soldiers in Iraq and Afghanistan. The events chronicled herein span the spectrum of participants from officers to noncommissioned officers and from combat units to support personnel, all in contact with a vicious and unforgiving enemy. CSI's authors made use of a variety of unclassified material and were able to contact and interview many of the key participants in each of these events. Each case study provides valuable insights for Soldiers and military professionals.

In Contact! is a companion to CSI's campaign histories of Operation IRAQI FREEDOM—*On Point* (2004), *On Point II* (due out in spring 2007), and a history of Operation ENDURING FREEDOM due out in mid-2008. *In Contact!* builds on the methods used in the widely distributed and renowned *Infantry in Battle* and *Seven Firefights in Vietnam*. As the Introduction explains, the format allows the case studies to be read as traditional narratives—following each case study from its initial situation, to its dilemma, through to its resolution. They can also be used in the Army school system as a teaching tool by having students read through the dilemma, then fostering student discussion and analysis of options before moving on to the actual historical conclusion.

As the long war continues around the world, the insights gained from this book will better prepare the Soldiers of the US Army for tomorrow's endeavors. Future volumes of this series will expand coverage of the Army's operations across the globe in the *Long War*. *CSI—The Past is Prologue!*

Timothy R. Reese
Colonel, Armor
Director, Combat Studies Institute

Contents

Maps

Figures

Introduction

by

William G. Robertson

Military historians have a wide range of choices when they come to address the history of a conflict. Some prefer to focus on the formulation of policy at the highest levels, where national military and political considerations intersect. Others choose to chronicle the purely strategic decisions made by senior military officers. Still another approach is represented by those who attempt to craft comprehensive chronological narratives, either of entire wars or discrete campaigns, most often from the perspective of the senior leaders involved. The biographical form represents an additional way to cover great events. All of these approaches involve telling the story in terms of a very few individuals at the higher echelons of power and influence. Standing in opposition to these categories is another genre of military history, which presents the worm's eye view of events as experienced by those in the ranks. Here first person accounts abound, usually delineating very low level and often mundane activities without placing them in a wider context. Often these first person accounts are gathered into a collective biography of a unit, but again context is often missing and the focus remains narrow. No matter whether the level at which the stories are told is high or low, the motives of their authors tend to fall within a relatively narrow range. Either the writer is simply chronicling events to preserve the historical record for the ages, or is attempting to provide analysis of key decisions, using copious amounts of hindsight. Both are noble endeavors, well within the canon of historical scholarship.

Either during or just after each of America's great conflicts of the past 100 years, a small subgenre of military historical writing has come into being, the discrete small unit narrative. Often couched as a case study, this type of work differs from the traditional approaches delineated above in several respects. Its focus is usually far below the policy level but somewhat above that of the individual Soldier. It places its subject within a wider context, but does not elaborate on that context. It rests on oral interviews more than on documents, although available documents are scrutinized for relevant facts. The enemy is only dimly seen, often because the conflict is still in progress or because his documents are not available. The treatment in no way is considered definitive. As such, the reasons for telling the story in this manner must be compelling to justify the effort. Those reasons tend to fall into two categories. First, if the conflict is still in progress, the author may simply wish to provide examples of heroic behavior or sacrifice for those serving in the midst of trying times, to rally the spirit and encourage emulation. A similar motivation can be applied to the American public at large, who have a right to know and, hopefully, appreciate the efforts of its military sons and daughters on its behalf. Second, the publication of such works represents a conscious effort to educate Soldiers in their profession. Looking at an event small enough for individuals to comprehend easily yet large enough to offer useful insights is a time-tested way to improve performance in those so educated. Sometimes this education is vicarious, provided to those who have not yet experienced similar events; for others, it may act more to reinforce knowledge already gained but perhaps forgotten. Either way, the primary purpose is to improve future performance. If the human spirit is lifted by the reading, well and good, but the practical, educational function is paramount.

In the midst of one of the United States Army's lowest periods in terms of end-strength, budget authority, and defined mission, prescient officers at the Infantry School, Colonel George C. Marshall and Major Forrest Harding, published a work in 1934 entitled *Infantry in Battle*. Consisting of a large number of case studies drawn from the American experience in World War I, the volume represented an effort to bridge the well-known gap between peacetime training experiences and the reality of combat. Designed as a text for use in the Army school system, *Infantry in Battle* offered a way for officers to prepare themselves vicariously for fiery trials ahead. The format proved so popular that the work quickly became a classic. Indeed, its form has been replicated in large measure by a work of the same title published in 2005, which draws on vignettes from the ongoing war on terrorism. Following World War II, the War Department Historical Division in 1946 published *Small Unit Actions*, the study of four discrete battles drawn from three diverse theaters of war. While the educational motive was present to some degree, the primary purpose of this volume was to explain to all, public and Soldiers alike, what the recent war looked like at battalion level and below. In 1954, following the Korean War, the Office of the Chief of Military History, United States Army, published *Combat Actions in Korea*. Consisting of descriptions of 19 small unit actions, this substantial volume found its primary justification as an educational tool for those who had not experienced the events described. Fully annotated, each chapter consisted of a colorful narrative followed by an analytical discussion of salient points. Nearly 20 years later, toward the end of American combat in Vietnam, the Office of the Chief of Military History again essayed to address small unit actions with the publication of *Seven Firefights in Vietnam*. This work aspired only to provide straightforward narratives that were representative of the types of combat American

Soldiers had encountered in that conflict. Based on primary sources but without annotation in the published version, the chapters were also devoid of overt analysis, which was left to the reader.

The present volume lies directly within the tradition of the predecessor works on small unit actions cited earlier. Since the fall of 2001, the Armed Forces of the United States of America have been engaged in a war on terrorism whose end is currently not in sight. Like World War II, that conflict has battlefronts that are geographically diverse and widely divergent in troops available and methods used. Because the war has so many different fronts and facets, no handful of small unit case studies could do justice to such a complex tapestry of events. This book thus represents only the first volume in a series of works that will showcase the American Soldier in both "lethal" and "nonlethal" operations in the war on terrorism. These first seven case studies are drawn from events in both Iraq and Afghanistan, two of the principal fronts in the war. Six of the chapters are drawn from the US Army's experience in Iraq, following the end of the conventional phase of the conflict, and represent small unit actions taking place as part of the effort to stabilize that war-torn country. The remaining chapter is set in Afghanistan and represents a similar small unit situation in a slightly different geographical context. In each case, the story is derived from oral interviews and key documents and is fully annotated. The cases vary from battalion-size operations to squad-level fights and the actions of individual Soldiers. They include both Regular Army and National Guard formations, emphasizing that the war on terrorism requires the involvement of the Total Army. Each of the cases terminated successfully, but none was without cost. All involved heroism and raw courage of the highest order, and in that regard all Americans should be proud of what their fellow citizens have done for the cause of freedom. Nevertheless, the primary purpose of presenting these case studies is the same as most of the preceding volumes, to provide a vicarious education in what future participants will face as the war on terrorism continues.

Because of the primary educational focus of this work, all seven case studies have been crafted in a particular way. After setting the context in which the action transpires, each chapter in its narrative section focuses on a protagonist, someone who will face a dilemma. That dilemma is overtly stated, and the possible courses of action open to the protagonist are detailed and analyzed. At that point, a paragraph break is introduced in the text to permit the story of the protagonist, the dilemma, and the possible courses of action to be separated physically from what follows. Thus, for instructional purposes, this material can be provided to either individuals or groups for thought, analysis, and discussion without knowledge of the outcome prejudicing the debate. Beyond the paragraph break, the course of action adopted by the protagonist is described, followed by the resolution of the situation and any analytical points the individual author has chosen to make. In no instance do these case studies represent the last word in historical terms on the subjects addressed. Instead, they represent no more than an interim snapshot of a discrete event, with only enough facts presented to prompt reflection, discussion, and understanding. Readers in the quiet of their study or the collegial atmosphere of the classroom will have the twin luxuries of time and a benign environment in which to assess the various situations presented and evaluate the choices made by the protagonists. That assessment should be conducted with a single end in view—to train the mind to perform better in the future. We cannot learn if we do not assess, but we must assess with humanity. If this work assists future professionals to do both, it will have succeeded in its goal.

6 November 2006

Shootout on Objective WOLF, 10 November 2004

by

Matt M. Matthews

For a brief time after the fall of Saddam Hussein in the spring of 2003, the city of Fallujah remained one of the most peaceful in Al Anbar province. All too soon, however, insurgent violence engulfed the region, and in March 2004, four US contractors were killed and mutilated in Fallujah. The atrocity resulted in US Marines being ordered into the city to apprehend the assailants and put down the fast-growing insurgency. Operation VIGILANT RESOLVE, the first Marine assault on Fallujah, began on 5 April 2004. Confronted by roughly 300,000 civilians and 2,000 insurgents, the Marines were hard pressed from the beginning. After suffering heavy losses and decisively losing the information operations (IO) campaign, they were forced to call off the attack on the city. With the withdrawal of the Marines, Fallujah became an insurgent stronghold, reinforced by foreign fighters and insurgents from around the world.

In early September 2004, Multinational Corps–Iraq (MNC-I) ordered the 1st Marine Expeditionary Force (I MEF) to begin planning for a new assault on the insurgent bastion of Fallujah. By early November 2004, after persuading most of the civilian population to leave the city, the 1st Marine Division (1 MAR DIV) stood poised to renew their assault on the approximately 3,000 insurgents and foreign fighters who occupied Fallujah. Initially designated Operation PHANTOM FURY, the name was changed at the last minute to Operation AL FAJR (NEW DAWN) to more adequately reflect Iraqi partnership in the endeavor. The division's major combat components consisted of Regimental Combat Team-1 (RCT-1) and Regimental Combat Team-7 (RCT-7), which swept into the city from the north. Constrained by a lack of heavy-mechanized forces, 1 MAR DIV attached one US Army heavy task force to each regimental combat team. In the west, Task Force 2-7 (TF 2-7) led the way for RCT-1, while Task Force 2-2 (TF 2-2) attacked south through the eastern side of the city with two Marine battalions from RCT-7.[1] Once inside the city, A Company, Task Force 2-2 (A/2-2) would face 12 days of almost continuous combat marked by bravery, sacrifice, and daring leadership.

With 6 months to prepare for 1 MAR DIV's assault, the 3,000 insurgents and foreign fighters in Fallujah established a formidable defense. Trenches and berms encircled the city, while concrete barriers blocked main avenues within Fallujah itself. In and around Fallujah, the enemy placed all manner of improvised explosive devices (IEDs), vehicle-borne improvised explosive devices (VBIEDs), and mines. Insurgents and foreign fighters also built extensive strongpoints and bunkers inside buildings throughout the city. Armed with large quantities of rocket propelled grenades (RPGs), mortars, rockets, and small arms, the enemy turned the city into an intimidating stronghold.[2]

As the supporting effort for 1 MAR DIV, RCT-7 would attack into Fallujah from north to south with three battalions abreast. The 1st Battalion, 8th Marines (1/8) would assault into the city on RCT-7's western boundary with 1st Battalion, 3d Marines (1/3) to their east. TF 2-2 to the east of 1/3 Marines would launch their attack into eastern Fallujah as the supporting effort for RCT-7. TF 2-2's mission was to pierce the enemy's defenses and rapidly secure Highway 10, or Phase Line (PL) FRAN as it was identified on 1 MAR DIV's control graphics. This was an important mission inasmuch as Highway 10 provided the only viable means to supply RCT-7 once it entered the city. The RCT-7's plan also called for TF 2-2 to secure the industrial area of southeast Fallujah and included an on-order mission to conduct search and attack operations toward the southwest.[3]

LTC Peter A. Newell, commander of TF 2-2, was an experienced combat leader known for his composed demeanor, even in the most harrowing circumstances. Although considered reticent by some, he was extremely well liked by his men. For this operation, his task force consisted of A Company, 2d Battalion, 2d Infantry Regiment (A/2-2); A Company, 2d Battalion, 63d Armor Regiment (A/2-63); and F Troop, 4th Cavalry Regiment (F/4CAV), also known as the brigade reconnaissance team (BRT). Newell's force also included the task force scouts and mortars as well as two M109A6s (155-mm Paladins). The Paladins were attached to TF 2-2 to ensure the unit possessed a destructive and precise indirect fire capability. Providing the bulk of the task force's firepower was 14 M1A1 tanks and 16 M2A2 Bradleys.[4] An Iraqi battalion, 2d Battalion Iraqi Intervention Force (2BN/IIF), was also assigned to TF 2-2 and would follow Newell's unit into the city.

It was readily apparent that without a breach of the expansive railroad berm on the north side of the city, TF 2-2 would not be able to move its tanks and Bradleys into Fallujah. For the assault, Newell assigned A/2-2 the task of opening this major obstacle. A/2-2's commander, CPT Sean P. Sims, was described as "a quiet and thoughtful leader" and was highly respected by the Soldiers in his company.[5] Sims' executive officer was 1LT Edward D. Iwan, a former enlisted man and one of the most popular officers in A/2-2.[6] Sims' company contained 1LT Jeff Emery's 1st Platoon (1/A/2-2) and 1LT Joaquin Meno's 3d Platoon (3/A/2-2). Both of these platoons were Bradley platoons. 2LT Shawn Gniazdowski commanded 2d Platoon, which was an engineer platoon from A Company, 82d Engineer Battalion (2/A/82EN). Gniazdowski's platoon was equipped with a mine-clearing line charge (MCLIC) for the breaching operation. The 4th Platoon was the tank platoon, commanded by 1LT Brian Hartman. Hartman's platoon had been attached from B Company, 1st Battalion, 63d Armor Regiment (4/B/1-63).

Meno had recently branch-transferred from the Adjutant Generals Corps to the infantry and assumed leadership of 3d Platoon (3/A/2-2), replacing the former leader, a West Point graduate and Ranger. Meno was well liked by his men who considered him a "stud" and "a kid with heart who listened to his NCOs [noncommissioned officers]."[7] It was the new leader's good fortune to work with a remarkable group of NCOs: SFC James Cantrell, platoon sergeant; SSG Scott Lawson, weapons' squad leader; SSG Colin Fitts, who had rejoined his unit after sustaining gunshot wounds to both arms and a knee in April, first squad assault leader; and SSG David Bellavia, second squad assault leader.[8]

Raised in western New York State, Bellavia enlisted in the Army in 1999, signing up for the infantry. "It was a tough go as far as finding steady work and things to do, so I joined the Army," Bellavia remembered. Regarded by those in his company as a man of diverse interests who could debate world history and politics,[9] Bellavia had already distinguished himself as a courageous combat leader. In the 8 months he and his platoon had served in Iraq, they had experienced major firefights and close quarters urban combat. When asked by a Marine if they were ready to assault the city, Bellavia replied, "Yeah, we're ready."[10] So in the early evening of 8 November 2004, Bellavia found himself in the back of a Bradley Fighting Vehicle (BFV) north of Fallujah waiting for the assault to begin.

At 1714, CPT Paul Fowler's A/2-63 moved from its attack position into its attack-by-fire location on the outskirts of northeastern Fallujah to provide covering fire for the breaching operation. Calling artillery fire on enemy locations to his front, Fowler ordered his company to unleash three simultaneous volleys into the outermost buildings.[11] "It really felt like the end of the world," recalled Jane Arraf, war correspondent for CNN, as she watched the torrent of destruction descend on the city.[12]

Approximately 29 minutes later, A/2-2 rolled out of their attack position and Sims arrayed his platoons for crossing the line of departure (LD) and conducting the breaching operation. By 1841, Sims' tanks and Bradleys were pounding enemy locations and reported killing four insurgents. At 1850, Emery called for smoke to help obscure the breaching operation from the insurgents. Sims'company crossed the LD at exactly 1900. A minute later, as the company moved forward, an enemy mortar round exploded over Iwan's Bradley. As the insurgents' shells exploded around them and sniper bullets pinged off their vehicles, Sims moved his company forward.

The A/2-2 commander directed his engineer platoon to the site he had personally selected for the breach. Still under continuous fire from the insurgents, Gniazdowski's engineer platoon fired their MCLIC. The resulting explosion caused the detonation of five or more IEDs—the detonations clearly visible for miles. By 1925, the breach was complete and within 15 minutes the lead elements of A/2-2 maneuvered their M1A1s and M2A2s through the opening and into the city, securing a foothold on Objective LION. By all accounts the initial breaching operation was a huge success, allowing A/2-2 to claim the honor of being the first unit in 1 MAR DIV to enter the city. As A/2-2 probed south, Gniazdowski's engineers continued making improvements to the breach.[13]

At 2013, A/2-63 moved through A/2-2's breach (see map 1) and headed several hundred yards straight west toward Objective LEOPARD. On Objective LION, Sims' company killed six insurgents and began moving directly south toward Objective PANTHER. The Iraqi soldiers of 2BN/IIF started moving through the breach at 2200. The Iraqis were forced to move through the breach dismounted, as their two-wheel-drive trucks could not maneuver over the top of the fractured railroad tracks. TF 2-2's CSM, Steve Faulkenburg, who had been following A/2-63, grew concerned with the delay and ordered his driver to turn his Humvee around and return to the breach site. As Faulkenburg exited the vehicle to help ground-guide his driver through the darkened, rubble-strewn street, a bullet hit Faulkenburg above his right eyebrow killing him instantly.[14] Less than 5 hours into the fight, Newell's senior NCO was dead; this loss hit TF 2-2 hard. Bellavia told a reporter, "There wasn't one fight we had when I didn't see him there, spitting Red Man through his stained teeth."[15]

By 0030 on 9 November, Sims' company reached Objective PANTHER. At 0106, as Meno's platoon started moving south toward Objective COUGAR it began to take small arms fire from Objective WOLF. A/2-2 and 2BN/IIF secured Objective COUGAR at 0403. Leaving 2BN/IIF at Objective COUGAR, Sims' continued moving elements of his company west toward Objective WOLF. At 0600, A/2-2 blasted its way onto Objective WOLF, the men confident they had destroyed the enemy on the objective. During the fight from the breach site to Objective WOLF, A/2-2 sustained three wounded Soldiers. Although the fight through

8

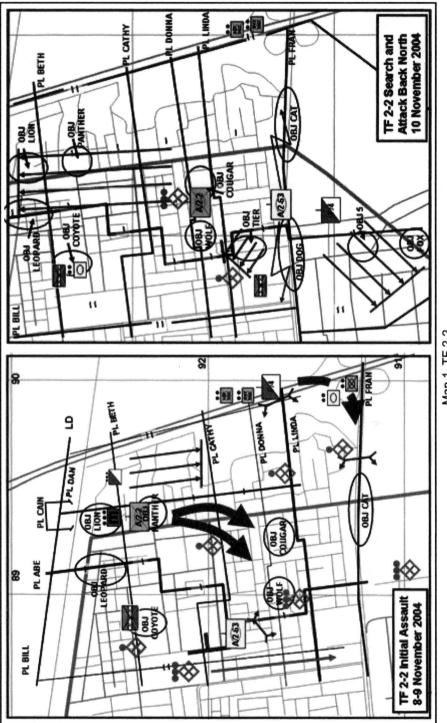

Map 1. TF 2-2.

northeastern Fallujah often involved dismounted clearing operations, A/2-2's casualties were surprisingly light. After repelling an insurgent counterattack near Objectives WOLF and COUGAR, Sims' exhausted company was allowed a tactical pause to rearm and resupply along Phase Line LINDA at 0610. One hour and ten minutes later, A/2-2 began driving toward its main objective—PL FRAN.

At approximately 0730, TF 2-2 reached PL FRAN. With A/2-63 to their west and the BRT to their east, A/2-2 maneuvered onto the highway. "When we hit PL FRAN it was chaotic and stupid for at least 20 minutes," Emery remembered. "We were on the highway and now we were exposed to everything." Indeed, as the Bradleys and tanks on PL FRAN scanned south, and as the 1st and 3d Platoons of A/2-2 began to drop off dismounted infantry to clear buildings north of the highway, insurgents on the south side of the road unleashed an immense salvo of RPGs and small arms fire. "That's when I remember the RPGs flying left and right," Emery acknowledged. "I remember counting the RPGs impacting buildings . . . they were actually impacting . . . where we had troops and they were impacting pretty close to the vehicles."[16] Within minutes, Newell and his company commanders were calling in artillery and blasting enemy positions south of the highway with direct fire, effectively neutralizing the insurgents. By 0909, TF 2-2 secured a foothold south of Highway 10. With the Marine units following them hindered by heavy fighting, TF 2-2's Soldiers found themselves far in advance of the rest of RCT-7. As a result of the Marines' delay, Newell's command was ordered to hold at PL FRAN and wait for the Marines to reach their flanks.

At 0645 on 10 November, A/2-63 assumed the security mission on PL FRAN. While A/2-2 was conducting search and attack missions north of PL FRAN, the insurgents who had concealed themselves in houses and spider holes during the night were making their presence felt behind TF 2-2. Meno's 3d Platoon was assigned the task of clearing from PL FRAN northward to PL LINDA, while Emery's 1st Platoon was ordered to conduct clearing operations all the way back to the LD. Gniazdowski's engineer platoon along with the TF 2-2 Scout Platoon would search for the enemy along the eastern sector between PL FRAN and PL LINDA. As the day wore on, A/2-2 made steady progress in rooting out bypassed insurgents. At 1610, Iwan reported the capture of a large group of insurgents near Objective WOLF, a residential area consisting of mostly upper middle class homes. As 14 enemy fighters waving white flags came out the front of the building, 6 to 8 insurgents with AK47s and RPGs ran out the back. When Iwan attempted to engage the fleeing insurgents from his Bradley, his 25-mm cannon malfunctioned. Cordoning off the area, Iwan ordered 3d Platoon to check all 12 buildings in the area and either kill or capture the enemy. Michael Ware, a correspondent for *Time* magazine and part of a large contingent of reporters traveling with TF 2-2, had attached himself to 3d Platoon. As he would later recall, "It seemed clear to me—and certainly to the men of 3d Platoon, these combatants were choosing to stand, fight, and most surely die."[17] At 1730, Meno's 3d Platoon began their search.

At 0145, 11 November, after clearing nine buildings and finding AK47s, RPGs, ammunition and flak vests but no insurgents, Fitts led his squad along with four Soldiers from Bellavia's squad into the tenth house. Bellavia remembered the front door was open, which should have caused some suspicion.[18] Ware recalled the 3d Platoon "in a long file entering the concrete-roof carport and small garden," and then moving through the front door. Ware and several Soldiers remained outside the home. Entering the house on the ground floor, Fitts' squad turned left and quickly cleared the first room. As the squad entered the second room, two insurgents under a stairwell and well protected by a concrete wall unleashed a barrage of automatic weapons fire. As bullets ripped through the wall, several Soldiers were wounded by shards of glass and other airborne fragments. One round penetrated a Soldier's body armor causing a minor wound to his side. As Fitts' men attempted to fire at the insurgents under the stairwell, gunfire erupted from the adjacent kitchen as insurgents began firing out the window into the carport and garden. "Rounds came out the windows," Ware stated, "and began hitting the iron gate behind me and the Soldiers. Concrete chips came off the pillars. Fragments from the rounds and the iron gate were flying everywhere."[19]

With bullets shredding the interior of the house, insurgents shooting wildly from the kitchen, and Fitts' men trapped, Bellavia sprang into action. Near the front of the house, Bellavia seized an M249 Squad Automatic Weapon (SAW) from one of his men and entered the doorway of the room where Fitts and his squad were pinned down. With enemy rounds striking the wall and doorway around him, Bellavia released a torrent of bullets at the two insurgents under the stairwell, effectively suppressing their fire. As the two insurgents scrambled for cover, Fitts' squad ran from the house and out into the street.

"Every face was cut with glass and metal," Bellavia remembered.[20] Ware recalled, "There was a lot of panic, a lot of confusion. No one knew what to do."[21] As Bellavia and Fitts performed a headcount of their bleeding men, insurgents on the roof of the house opened fire on them. With rounds impacting around them, Fitts ordered some of his men into an overwatch position in a house across the street while others in the platoon sought the safety of the wall surrounding the house. From behind the wall a young private yelled out, "We're all going to die." Bellavia firmly responded, "We're not going to die."[22]

Bellavia called for a Bradley, which rolled up immediately in front of the house. Behind the Bradley, Bellavia, Fitts, Ware, and Meno took stock of their situation. "It was at this point," Ware recalled, "I witnessed SSG Bellavia begin to take control of the situation. The platoon had been shocked and was clearly rattled by the close quarters ambush. There was great confusion. No one could tell where the enemy was or in what strength. . . . Bellavia began shouting to the Soldiers in 3d Platoon to encourage them and give them a rallying point, being himself."[23] With Bellavia's help, it took Meno approximately 7 minutes to restore order to his platoon. Having stabilized the situation, Meno quickly moved more of his men into the house across the street from the enemy.

Bellavia ordered the Bradley crew to open fire on the house, but the high walls surrounding the home made it impossible to strike anything but the corner of the kitchen. As the gunner tried in vain to find a better shot, insurgents once again opened fire from the shelter of the house. Ware stated, "I do not believe anyone wanted to go back inside that house which, for all intents and purposes, seemed like a death trap with all the advantages in the enemy's favor. . . . The situation demanded decisive action."[24] Although indirect fire support and close air support (CAS) were available, each option would take time and would require the dismounted infantry to mount their Bradleys and back out of the area. Meno could have organized his men and launched an assault on the insurgents' position, but he needed time to prepare his traumatized platoon. He could have called on one of the nearby tanks for assistance, but it appeared immediate action was warranted and deployment of a tank would take time. Meno could also have elected to await instructions from his company commander, Sims.

*   *   *

As the insurgents' bullets continued to pelt the street around him, Bellavia stated, "I became livid."[25] Grabbing an M16A4, he proceeded toward the front of the house. Ware remembered Bellavia "pacing like a caged animal in the street.[26] I saw SSG Bellavia stop pacing as though he'd made a decision. He turned and called out, 'Hey strike team, on me.' No one moved and he remained standing alone. SSG Bellavia then called again, 'My squad get on me now.' Some Soldiers taking cover nearby

12

responded inaudibly, but they did not move. Bellavia took a few steps toward them and motioning to the Soldiers asked, 'That new ammo? Let's go, let's go. Who's got more ammo?'"[27] Finally, Lawson, the weapons squad leader for 3d Platoon, and another Soldier joined Bellavia in the street. As the three men moved toward the back of the Bradley, another Soldier dashed across the street to join them. Ware, who was also behind the Bradley, heard Bellavia say, "I want to go in there and go after them." One of the Soldiers threw a grenade over the wall. After the resulting explosion, all five men ran back through the gate, across the carport, and up to one of the windows of the house.

Assigning two Soldiers to watch the corners of the home, Bellavia started for the front door. Lawson told Bellavia, "You are not going in there to die alone." Taken aback by Lawson's bravado, Bellavia asked, "You're f___ coming?" As the two men entered the house, Ware brought up the rear. Turning to Ware, Bellavia ordered him to "Get the f___ out!" Ware refused to leave, and told Bellavia, "I can't let you go. This is the most amazing thing I have ever seen! You're an American hero."[28]

In the house (see figure 1), which was eerily illuminated by burning pieces of paper and smoldering walls, Bellavia could hear the insurgents whispering behind the wall of the second room near the stairwell. Advancing toward the room, Bellavia ordered Ware to run if gunfire erupted. Ignoring the danger, the reporter followed Bellavia into the second room. Gunfire erupted almost immediately as Bellavia traded shots with the insurgents near the stairwell. Peering into the room, he saw an enemy fighter firing an RPK light machine gun and another loading an RPG. Bellavia immediately engaged the insurgents under the stairwell shooting and killing the one with the RPG. As the other enemy fighter fired and ran toward the kitchen, Bellavia shot him in the shoulder. Turning to Ware he said, "I could see their eyes, and there was no fear. I'll never forget those eyes."[29] Outside the house, Soldiers could hear the insurgent screaming in pain from the kitchen. In the midst of the shouting from the house, Bellavia and Ware heard yet another insurgent yelling from the second floor.

Responding to the gunfire, Lawson ran into the hallway and joined Bellavia. Armed with only a 9-mm pistol, Lawson blasted away at the kitchen door while the still-screaming enemy fighter behind the door opened fire with an AK47. As both men fired round after round through the door, a large fragment of either the door or the wall hit Lawson's right shoulder. Bellavia remembered Lawson "beating his leg" in anger and "shooting the dead guy on the ground." With Lawson injured and down to his last magazine, Bellavia ordered him out of the house. As Lawson

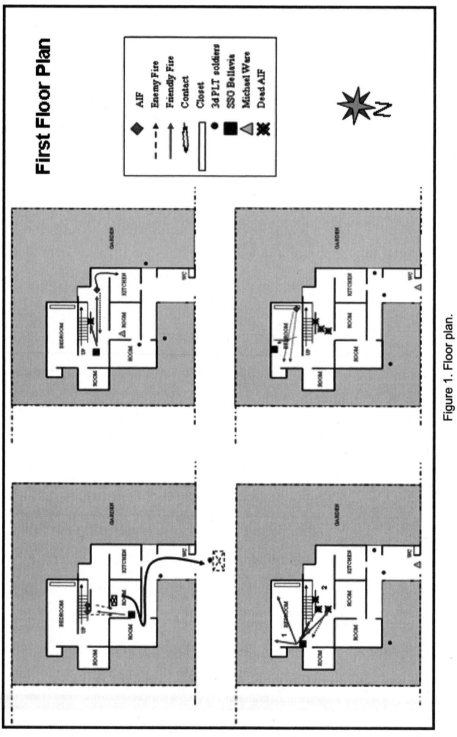

Figure 1. Floor plan.

scurried out, Bellavia told him to bring back a shotgun with buckshot and more men. Lawson yelled back, "don't go anywhere." Ware, who had stayed in the second room during the gun battle had already beaten a hasty retreat from the house taking up a position near the carport. During the lull, Bellavia called his platoon sergeant, Cantrell, on his radio. Cantrell, who was not with Meno, immediately responded yelling into the mike, "What the f___ are you doing," and demanding a situation report. From the carport, Ware heard Bellavia scream back, "I'm kind of a bit stressed right now! Just give me a moment and I'll let you know."[30]

To Bellavia's great consternation, he realized there was yet another room to his rear that he had not cleared. This was the master bedroom. As Bellavia peered through the doorway, he heard someone moving in the room. Firing into the corners of the bedroom, he noticed a large wardrobe with six doors on the west side of the room. As he attempted to orient himself, an insurgent charged down the stairs from the second floor, moved into the hallway, and began firing into the bedroom. Taking cover behind the wall near the doorway, Bellavia listened as another insurgent began screaming from the second floor. To his astonishment, yet another insurgent started screaming from somewhere in the master bedroom. Thinking quickly, Bellavia began to scan the room with his AN/PEQ-2A laser sight. Certain that an enemy fighter was hiding in the wardrobe, he began firing from left to right into each door. Before he could place his last shot into the sixth and final door, the wounded insurgent in the kitchen made a mad dash across the hall and began pumping rounds from his AK47 into the bedroom. As the enemy fire ripped through the doorframe, Bellavia fired back and moved briskly to the east corner of the master bedroom. When the insurgent from the kitchen approached the bedroom doorway and began to fire, Bellavia wounded the man in the left breast with one shot. A split second later, Bellavia fired again killing him instantly.[31]

Scanning the bedroom, Bellavia realized a door to the wardrobe was now ajar. Suddenly, tracer fire erupted from the wardrobe, the rounds impacting against the far wall. At that moment, the insurgent from the second floor reappeared, showering the bedroom with bullets. As he appeared in the doorway, Bellavia fired, mortally wounding him. Writhing in pain, the insurgent crawled away from the door.[32]

While Bellavia attempted to catch his breath, all manner of clothing flew out of the wardrobe followed closely by an insurgent firing an AK47. Bellavia recalled his night vision goggles flying off his head as he turned and the sound of the gunfire piercing his ears as a large wooden splinter hit him in the shoulder. As he emerged from hiding, the enemy fighter tripped on the base of the wardrobe, causing it to fall forward on its doors.

Firing in all directions, the insurgent jumped on the bed and promptly lost his footing on the wobbly mattress. As he fell, Bellavia pumped several rounds into him. The man collapsed near the front door of the bedroom but still managed to fire a volley into the wall, barely missing Bellavia's head. Bleeding from his gunshot wounds, the enemy fighter began shouting in crude but decipherable English. From the second floor, an insurgent responded in Arabic. Bellavia recalled yelling back in Arabic "in an attempt to intimidate the men into surrendering."[33] To frighten Bellavia, the insurgents taunted him in English, saying "they would bury me in a Jewish cemetery with Jews, dogs will eat you, and we are coming to get you."[34] Having recently viewed the remake of the film *The Exorcist*, Bellavia recalled a line from the movie that he kept repeating over-and-over in his head, "The power of Christ compels you, the power of Christ compels you." Despite his many wounds, the insurgent near the doorway stood up and ran out of the master bedroom and up the stairs. Bellavia fired at the man, but missed.

Bellavia sprang to his feet and followed the insurgent out the door and up the stairs. As he hit the first flight of stairs, Bellavia slipped in a pool of blood. At the precise moment he fell forward, a volley from an AK47 ripped over his head. Catching sight of his foe on the first landing, Bellavia dove for cover as the wounded insurgent fired wildly down the stairs, riddling the stairwell with bullets. When the firing subsided, Bellavia charged up the stairs to the second floor following the blood trail to a room. Sensing someone in the room, Bellavia threw in a fragmentation grenade, which hit the insurgent in the head and fell to the floor. The blast ripped the right side of the insurgent's body, forcing him out onto the second story roof. On the rooftop he leapt up and down screaming, firing his AK47 indiscriminately into the house and out into the garden until he ran out of ammo. Crawling back into the smoke-filled room, the insurgent continued to pull the trigger of his empty weapon.

As the smoke from a burning mattress engulfed the room, Bellavia detected the smell of natural gas. Glancing quickly around the room, he identified a propane tank in the corner. At that moment, he heard two more insurgents shouting from the third floor. Fearful of an explosion, Bellavia put the insurgent who had just clambered back into the room in a chokehold. As the man fought back savagely, Bellavia hit him with his M16A4, swinging it like a baseball bat. As he swung, the enemy fighter countered hitting Bellavia in the side of the head and cracking his front tooth. During the struggle, the insurgent managed to draw a .45-caliber pistol. As they fought, the gun went off, the round slamming into the wall. Bellavia remembered firing two rounds at the man, but was uncertain as to whether he hit him. With his helmet loosened by the blow to his head, Bellavia removed it and brought it down several times on the insurgent's skull. As the man screamed in pain, Bellavia jumped on his stomach, and the man went limp for a brief moment. Bellavia distinctly remembered the man's putrid breath as the air was forced from his lungs.[35]

As Bellavia straddled the man, the insurgent continued to scream and bit into Bellavia's left hand. Convinced he was yelling instructions to the other insurgents, Bellavia tore open his armored vest and beat the man with his front Small Arms Protective Insert (SAPI) plate. As the insurgent began to wail, Bellavia warned him, "I don't want to kill you; shut your mouth." With the insurgent refusing to comply, and hearing footsteps on the floor above, Bellavia pulled out his Gerber tactical knife. As he did so, the insurgent bit him again. As Bellavia attempted to slit the insurgent's throat, his pain was compounded as the knife sliced into his little finger. Cupping his hand over the insurgent's mouth, Ballavia stabbed the insurgent in the left side of the throat. According to the packet nominating Bellavia for the Medal of Honor, "Bellavia bled the insurgent with applied pressure as he spastically kicked and scratched. . . ."[36]

From their overwatch position in the house across the street, Meno and the rest of 3d Platoon continued to monitor the situation. Meno recalled talking with Sims on the radio and updating him on their situation, while trying to obtain information from Cantrell, his platoon sergeant.[37] "I heard the exchange of more fire from the upper floor," Ware, the *Time* magazine reporter, remembered. "Then a long silence. One of the Soldiers next to me said to the other, 'We gotta find out if Sergeant Bell is okay.'" Ware then heard a whispered voice from near the front door of the house. "I didn't understand the word being whispered until the Soldier next to me said it was his name being whispered. A message that SSG Bellavia was not answering and more men were needed was then shouted to the rest of the platoon in their positions . . . across the street. I then heard SSG Fitts stand up and tell the Soldiers around him, 'Let's go.'"[38]

Battered and stunned, Ballavia staggered out of the room and into the hall without his weapon. Without warning, an insurgent jumped from the third story roof onto the second story roof, dropping his AK47 as he landed. Looking at him from a window, Bellavia realized he had no weapon and ran back into the smoke-filled room. Grabbing his M16A4 and running back to the window, Bellavia saw the insurgent scrambling for his AK47. Firing rapidly, Bellavia shot the man in the lower back. Believing he was dead, Bellavia headed toward the roof. As he approached the entryway, he saw the insurgent he had just shot "straddling a water tank at the edge of the roof." Slapping in his last magazine, Bellavia unloaded every round into the insurgent's legs. He then headed back toward the smoking room to retrieve another weapon. As he did, the insurgent fell from the roof into the garden.

As Fitts and his squad joined Bellavia in the house, Meno received word from Sims that a CAS mission had been called in by an adjacent unit. Meno recalled:

> They were going to drop a Joint Direct Attack Munition (JDAM) at a target less than 400 meters away from our location. I immediately informed the Soldiers on the ground that we needed to consolidate, take cover and pull back from the objective. By the time we got consolidated, SSG Bellavia and the other Soldiers at the objective linked back up with the rest of the platoon and SSG Bellavia informed me that he killed four insurgents single handedly and mortally wounded the fifth. After the JDAM detonated, the platoon and I then entered the objective to search for the mortally wounded insurgent and consolidate the insurgents that were killed. The fifth insurgent couldn't be found, but upon consolidating the bodies of the dead insurgents I noticed that one of the insurgents had a deep cut in his throat with large amounts of blood on his shirt. I then asked SSG Bellavia to see his Gerber utility knife and it was covered with blood. . . . I then reported to my Company Commander that the objective was cleared with four insurgents killed and the fifth mortally wounded. We were then instructed to take up a platoon strongpoint and maintain there over night.[39]

Unfortunately for A/2-2, the tumult was not over. The worst was yet to come. In the ensuing days, insurgents would kill both Company Commander Sims and Executive Officer Iwan. The courageous actions of Bellavia, however, did not go unnoticed. After leaving the Army and returning to New York State, Bellavia received a Silver Star in the mail. This momentous occasion, observed by only Bellavia and his mail carrier, was captured for all time by a simple snapshot.[40]

Notes

1. LTG John F. Sattler and LTC Daniel H. Wilson, "Operation AL FAJR: The Battle of Fallujah Part II," *Marine Corps Gazette*, July 2005, 12–24.

2. Bing West, *No True Glory: A Frontline Account of the Battle of Fallujah* (New York: Bantam Books, 2005), 256–257; Sattler and Wilson, "Operation AL FAJR," 14.

3. LTC Pete Newell, telephone interview by author, 23 March 2006.

4. TF 2-2 IN Operation PHANTOM FURY Summary, copy in author's file, no date.

5. Holly Huffman, "He was willing to make that sacrifice," *The Bryan-College Station Eagle*, 28 November 2004.

6. David Bellavia, "*American Hero: First Lieutenant Edward Iwan,*" online at <http://www.davidbellavia.com/american-heroes/edward-iwan/>, accessed 5 September 2006.

7. David Bellavia, telephone interview by author, 27 July 2006.

8. David Bellavia, e-mail to author, 28 July 2006; Bellavia interview, 27 July 2006.

9. Michael Ware, "Into the Hot Zone," *Time*, 22 November 2004, 32.

10. Bellavia interview, 27 July 2006.

11. Captain Paul Fowler, Memorandum for Record, Narrative of Combat Actions in Fallujah from 4 to 23 November 2004, dated 25 November 2004, copy in author's file.

12. Jane Arraf, telephone interview by author, 3 April 2006.

13. A Company Graphics from 8–12 November 2004, prepared by TF 2-2 staff, no date, copy in author's file; Narrative Recommendation for Award of the Silver Star to Captain Sean P. Sims, copy in author's file.

14. MAJ (Dr.) Lisa DeWitt, telephone interview by author, 23 April 2006.

15. Toby Harnden, "'The CO is dead' troops are told," *London Daily Telegraph*, 15 November 2006.

16. CPT Jeff Emery, telephone interview by author, 17 July 2006.

17. Michael Ware, "Inside the Insurgency," *Front Line*, Public Broadcasting Service, interview with Michael Ware, fall 2005.

18. Bellavia interview, 27 July 2006.

19. Michael Joseph Ware, DA Form 2823, Sworn Statement, "Statement Operation Dawn Fallujah, Iraq, November, 2004," 15 February 2005, Baghdad, Iraq, copy in author's file.

20. David Bellavia, telephone interview by author, 26 July 2006.

21. Ware interview, "Inside the Insurgency."

22. Bellavia interview, 27 July 2006.

23. Ware Sworn Statement.

24. Ibid.

25. Bellavia interview, 26 July 2006.

26. Ware interview, "Inside the Insurgency."

27. Ware Sworn Statement.

28. Bellavia interview, 26 July 2006.

29. Ware interview, "Inside the Insurgency."

30. Bellavia interview, 26 July 2006; Ware Sworn Statement.

31. Narrative Nominating SSG David Bellavia for the Medal of Honor During Operation PHANTOM FURY, copy in author's collection.

32. Ibid.

33. Ibid.

34. Bellavia interview, 26 July 2006.

35. Ibid.

36. Medal of Honor narrative.

37. 1LT Joaquin Manuel Meno, DA Form 2823, Sworn Statement, 8 December 2005, copy in author's file.

38. Ware Sworn Statement.

39. Meno Sworn Statement.

40. Bellavia interview, 26 July 2006.

American Advisor in Action, Mosul, 13 November 2004

by

Kendall D. Gott

The streets of Mosul, Iraq, in November 2004 were a battleground as insurgents fought to gain control of the city and undermine the interim government. There the 1st Brigade, 25th Infantry Division, assisted by Iraqi military and security units, attacked into the heart of the city to quickly defeat the insurgents, establish government control, and allow the scheduled elections to proceed. Pinned under a murderous crossfire during the melee, military advisor COL James H. Coffman, Jr., fought a battle of survival while attached to an Iraqi police commando unit sent to retake a captured police station near the center of Mosul. The decisions and actions he made that day would determine the success or defeat at the battle for the 4-West police station.

Astride the Tigris River about 400 kilometers north of Baghdad lies the ancient city of Mosul. With more than 1.7 million inhabitants, it is Iraq's third largest city, and the Tigris divides it into Kurdish and Arab halves. Under Saddam Hussein and the tradition of "Arabization" the Kurds continued to live around Mosul, and the dictator rewarded his loyal generals and cronies with estates. After the fall of Saddam Hussein, his sons sought refuge in Mosul and it became a violent and deadly place. Stranded Baathists and foreign jihadists formed an insurgency and sought to disrupt Coalition operations and the process of forming a new Iraqi government.

Coalition aircraft had intermittently targeted the military facilities and transportation infrastructure in and around Mosul in response to Iraq's repeated violations of United Nations' resolutions since 1991. The aftermath of Operation IRAQI FREEDOM in 2003 had brought further destruction and reduced much of Mosul to bombed-out, shot-up buildings by 2004. Although essential utilities such as water and electricity were operating sporadically, the populace lived in frustration and fear as the occupation and deadly attacks of terrorism continued.[1]

Insurgents planned attacks to disrupt the elections scheduled for January 2005 to select an Iraqi government to replace the interim administration. These attacks were also aimed to inflict casualties on the Coalition. If successful, the insurgents could create a shadow government, delay or discredit the elected Iraqi government, and perhaps even force the withdrawal of Coalition forces. When attacking the heavily armed forces of the

United States proved too costly, the insurgents shifted their focus. Instead of pitting themselves against the armor and firepower of the Americans, they sought to strike at softer targets with complete disregard for civilian casualties.

The insurgents found Iraqi policemen a lucrative opportunity in their campaign of attacks. On 26 June 2004, five Iraqi policemen were killed and eight injured when three suicide bombers detonated explosive devices at a guard station in the center of the city. These attacks became commonplace and increased as the American presidential and Iraqi national elections approached. The insurgents attacked 12 police stations in Mosul in a coordinated offensive on 10 November 2004, overrunning many of them and establishing control of large portions of Mosul. The credibility of the interim government and the ability of the people to vote in the elections were in the balance.

In 2004, the interim Iraqi government was in flux as various political and tribal elements vied for power. Confounding the process of forming a permanent government was the active and deadly insurgency. The pace of raising a standing competent army proved slow and gave rise to a number of hastily organized paramilitary organizations. Some of these organizations were formed under the auspices of the Ministry of Interior and Ministry of Defense, but numerous militias remained under local or tribal influence. Some of these units were successful in maintaining security while many were not. One successful endeavor was the creation of two police commando battalions in September 2004 and at least four more in the months that followed.

With a growing organizational strength that would eventually total more than 4,000 men, the commandos were under the overall command of General Adnan Thavit, the uncle of the interim Interior Minister. These commando battalions, with approximately 300 men each, fell outside of the Iraqi military hierarchy and instead reported directly to the Interior Ministry. Their primary mission was to establish security in the large cities by hunting down insurgents. Reliable recruits were chosen based on their technical background and loyalty to the nation of Iraq. Many had prior police experience, and others had previously served in the army or other security forces under the old regime. The police commandos were lightly armed, principally with AK47 rifles, RPG-7 rocket grenade launchers, pistols, and a few light mortars.[2]

The Multinational Security Transition Command-Iraq (MNSTC-I), commanded by LTG David II. Petraeus, was an organization established by the Coalition to provide support and training of police and other security force units. MNSTC-I reported directly to Central Command. A branch of this organization was the Civilian Police Assistance Training Team (CPATT), which was formed in May 2004 and tasked to monitor and assist the paramilitary units like the commandos. Heading this training team as senior advisor was Coffman. A graduate of the US Military Academy and a career Special Forces officer, Coffman had had a wide range of experiences and assignments over his 27-year career. The advisor team members and others who knew him described Coffman as a passionate, tough, no-nonsense warrior. As an advisor, Coffman focused on training and preparing the Ministry of Interior police forces to fight the insurgency. His role did not require participation in pitched battles, and he was not within the chain of command of any Iraqi unit. The cooperation from the Iraqis stemmed from his personality and the common objective of raising a viable counterinsurgency force.

When word of the formation of the commandos reached Coffman's team, he visited the facility in which they were housed. Coffman had seen a number of hastily organized Iraqi units over the past few months and he did not have high expectations of finding a newly raised unit ready for combat operations. His first impressions were not encouraging. The commandos of the 1st and 3d Battalions were living in very austere conditions in a heavily damaged former Republican Guards base outside of Baghdad. Utilities were scarce or nonexistent and the men were paid on an irregular basis. Unlike other Iraqi units he visited, however, Coffman was struck by the morale, discipline, and care for weapons and equipment that was lacking in some other Iraqi formations. Coffman convinced Petraeus to support the commandos with funds, vehicles, and equipment. This was a risky venture, as previous efforts to support paramilitary forces had not met with complete success. In some cases, the provided weapons and equipment found their way into the black market or into the hands of the insurgents.

Over the span of 9 weeks, their leaders forged the two Iraqi police commando battalions into a generally competent and disciplined force under the watchful eye of Coffman. Training was conducted beyond the mere firing of weapons and small unit tactics in urban terrain. The commandos were also trained to conduct raids, cordon-and-search, and to gather intelligence. The task of training recruits was far easier with these battalions than with many other paramilitary units in Iraq because these men had been very carefully screened and each trainee had some previous experience. Iraqi officers also were taught the techniques of coordinating supporting fires, air strikes, and logistics. The commandos' training and preparation was soon put to the test.

The religious holiday of Ramadan, which ran from mid-October through mid-November 2004, saw a substantial increase in insurgent activity throughout Iraq. Violence was particularly intense in Mosul, where on 10 November the insurgents specifically targeted the facilities of the Iraqi police and security forces. On that day, the insurgents attacked and overran all 12 of the police stations except for 1-West, the central police headquarters. Across the city, insurgents gunned down or chased away Iraqi police officers causing high casualties and damage. Observers of the fight were stunned by the discipline and organization showed by the attackers. This was not a motley assortment of terrorists, but a cohesive and dedicated force. Large areas of the city were soon under control of the insurgents who showed no signs of leaving. As long as they remained, there was no hope of conducting elections, and the prestige and legitimacy of the Iraqi interim government was in jeopardy.

COL Robert Brown's 1st Brigade, 25th Infantry Division had relieved the 3d Brigade, 2d Infantry Division in Mosul in January 2004 and by November had been conducting security operations for almost a year. This combat team consisted of a headquarters and headquarters company, three infantry battalions, an infantry antitank company, a cavalry reconnaissance squadron, a direct support field artillery battalion, a support battalion and separate engineer, and military intelligence and signal companies. The brigade had approximately 300 M1126 Stryker armored vehicles. At full strength, a Stryker brigade combat team numbered approximately 3,900 personnel. Although stationed in bases outside the city proper, the eight-wheeled 19-ton Stryker vehicles had become a common sight to the populace as the Soldiers acquired experience in the city while combating the insurgency. With the insurgent onslaught on 10 November, the battalions of the 1st Brigade prepared to launch coordinated attacks into the heart of the resistance to retake the city of Mosul.[3]

The Americans were not alone in their efforts to regain control of the streets of Mosul. Two Iraqi police commando battalions were alerted and moved by ground and air from their base near Baghdad to the embattled city on 12 November. In the early morning hours of 13 November, the two commando battalions arrived at the Mosul airfield near the southern outskirts where the air components of the coming operation were located. After a quick breakfast, the combined force moved into the city and quickly established a strong perimeter around the 1-West police station. No doubt the eight Iraqi policemen and squad of US military police defending the building were greatly relieved to see the friendly column arrive.

As the commandos secured the immediate area, the senior officers met to discuss options and plan the coming battle to retake the lost police stations. Major General Rashid Flaih, Commander of 1st Iraqi Special Police Brigade, chaired the meeting. Coffman and James Steele, the Counselor to the US Ambassador for Iraqi Security Forces, met with Brown to review the plan to reoccupy five strategic police stations within central Mosul. These meetings designated zones of operation, routes, logistics, rules of engagement, and coordinated fire and air support. The assault into Mosul by forces of about 1,600 Iraqi security forces, including the commandos, and 1,200 American Soldiers of the 1st Brigade, 25th Infantry Division was set for the following morning.[4]

The initial commando attack went well, apparently catching the insurgents off balance and quickly recapturing some of the police stations. In other parts of the city, the three Stryker battalions of the American 1st Brigade began their offensive. Advancing along multiple axes, this attack divided the insurgent's attention and resources to several threatened areas. The American method of attack limited the insurgents' ability to mass, and they were only able to rally in small groups and counterattack selected points. One of these was police station 4-West, where a commando platoon found itself pinned down by heavy fire and was in danger of being overrun.

With the command and staff preparations complete, Coffman attached himself to a quick reaction force (QRF) of the 3d Battalion, 1st Iraqi Special Police Commando Brigade. This force was positioned to deploy rapidly to assist friendly units in need of assistance or to exploit any opportunities that might arise. Captain Ahmed Abbas led the force that consisted of between 80 to 100 men. As an advisor and observer, Coffman was not expected to engage in direct combat operations but to lend technical assistance and to advise the Iraqi commander if needed. To do more could seriously undermine the unit's chain of command and cause serious repercussions between the United States and the interim government of Iraq. Coffman was armed with his M4 carbine and wore protective body armor, but both were intended only for personal protection. Receiving a call for help from the garrison of the embattled 4-West police station around 1200, the reaction force with Coffman was sent into the heart of Mosul and deep into the area controlled by the insurgents.

When the commando vehicle column was about 100 meters short of the 4-West station, it was ambushed in a sudden hail of rocket-propelled grenades, small arms fire, and mortar rounds (see map 2). The commandos quickly jumped from their vehicles and took what little cover there was available in the urban canyon. Bullets riddled abandoned vehicles and

RPG-7 grenades hit two. The streets filled with oily smoke from burning trucks, explosions, and automatic rifle fire; screams from the wounded added to the chaos. The insurgents, dressed in black tracksuits and ski masks, were well equipped and disciplined. They selected good firing positions and expertly coordinated their ambush from rooftops and windows and had cut-off and surrounded the commandos. The commandos pinned down under such fire had but two options—fight or flee. Even veteran troops would have been hard pressed to remain fighting in such a predicament, but the commandos remarkably held their composure. Still, they were not invincible, and with most of their officers down, the Iraqis were in danger of breaking.[5]

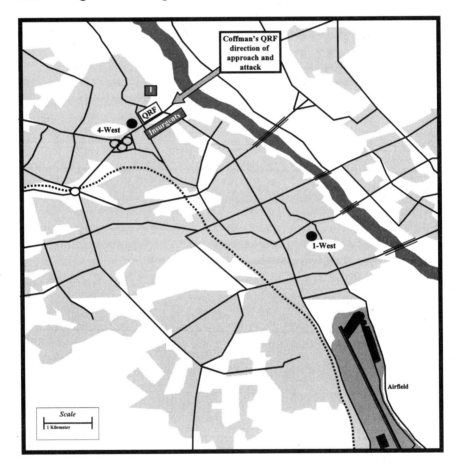

Map 2. Commandos ambushed.

Coffman faced a dilemma. He had accompanied the commandos as an observer, and as such, he was not within their chain of command and (technically) had no authority over them. However, with the Iraqi officers killed or wounded, the situation was rapidly deteriorating. Coffman could have assisted the senior NCO still on his feet, but was unable to identify him in the chaos of the moment. A direct attempt to take command would come at great risk, because he would have to expose himself to enemy fire to execute that function. Faced with a significant language barrier, Coffman had no guarantee the Iraqi commandos would understand what he wanted done. Indeed, there was no certainty they would be willing to follow him even if he made that decision. For his trouble, the Iraqi interim government could well take offense at an American acting so presumptuously, and the matter would become an international incident. On the other hand, retreat would be a hazardous affair for the virtually surrounded commandos and require abandoning their killed and wounded comrades. Although choosing that option could save Coffman's own life, it could well end the rapport he had with the commandos and weaken the stature of the Civilian Police Assistance Training Team in the eyes of the Iraqis. The situation demanded an immediate decision.

*   *   *

Assessing the desperate situation quickly, Coffman personally rallied the remaining commandos while trying to radio for assistance. These actions were technically beyond the charter of an advisor, but with the commando leaders down, Coffman's experience and training kicked in to save the remaining Iraqis from annihilation. Not fluent in their language, he moved from commando to commando under heavy fire, looking each in the eye and using hand and arm signals to demonstrate what he wanted done. Coffman also demonstrated to all what was required by personal example, engaging the enemy and tenaciously holding his position. In these moments, he was able to solidify a defense and bolster the determination of the commandos to hold their positions, while protecting their wounded comrades. There they would fight and die until relieved or victorious. The battle for the streets raged unabated as small groups of commandos held their exposed and scattered positions under heavy fire.

Casualties mounted gradually as the insurgents occasionally found their mark. Fortunate to escape injury during the initial ambush, Coffman's luck ran out about an hour into the fight when an enemy round shattered his shooting hand and damaged his carbine. After bandaging his wound, Coffman grabbed a nearby AK47 rifle from a fallen commando and continued to fight. Unable to insert another magazine into the weapon because of his injuries, he simply dropped the rifle and picked up another from a nearby commando casualty. With a burst of adrenaline and pain numbed by shock, Coffman was able to operate fully a third AK47 he acquired and went through several magazines of ammunition. The commandos near him responded by fighting with renewed energy and tossed him more ammunition to fire. With the men fighting vigorously, Coffman and an assisting Iraqi comrade distributed ammunition to the uninjured commandos, exposing themselves repeatedly to enemy fire. When all that remained were loose rounds, Coffman held magazines between his legs and loaded the rounds with his good hand.

Coffman continued to rally the remaining commandos while trying to radio for assistance. For 4 hellish hours, they repulsed attack after attack by the enemy. At one point, the insurgents made a desperate assault and came within 20 meters of Coffman's position. ". . . I had to beat them back by firing. Most of the guys around me were wounded and pinned down. There wasn't really much cover so we were just trying to stay out of sight." Coffman and the commandos were still fighting, but casualties were high and supplies of ammunition were low. Of nine men in Coffman's position, all were wounded or dead except for one soldier who was miraculously unscathed. "One guy took it in the leg and just eventually bled out in spite of our efforts to stop the bleeding. The guy next to me got hit in the neck and it came out through his cheek so I helped treat him."[6] A nearby position held four commandos with two of them seriously wounded. That situation was typical in each group of commandos. Pinned down by fire, some had no chance for escape and the commandos who did have an egress route refused to abandon their comrades.

With the commandos nearly out of ammunition, the situation was grim. Fortunately, the commandos of QRF-2, under the personal command of Flaih, arrived on the scene at approximately 1600. This company-size unit was formed from elements of the 3d Commando Battalion and had spent the morning assisting Iraqi units in contact, moving from one fight to another as needed. Hearing the noise of the battle several blocks away, Flaih had simply moved his unit to the sound of the heaviest fighting. Coffman led the general and his unit to his position and assisted in organizing the arriving commando forces. When told to go to the rear for medical treatment, Coffman refused stating his intention to remain until the fight was over. (See map 3.)

Air support became available not long after the arrival of QRF-2, and additional reinforcements soon arrived in the form of C Company, 3d Battalion, 21st Infantry Regiment from the 1st Brigade, 25th Infantry

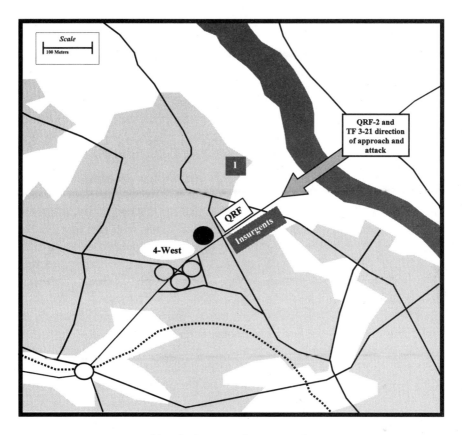

Map 3. Commandos rescued.

Division. The insurgents did not break and run even after the arrival of the American Stryker vehicles. Instead, they tried to flank the commando positions, but got between them and the arriving quick reaction forces. Heavy ordnance from both air and ground was quickly applied to the buildings and positions occupied by the insurgents. Caught in the crossfire, the insurgents finally began to fall back. Coffman remained in action to direct air strikes and to provide vital information on the location of enemy and friendly forces to the commander of the Stryker unit, LTC Michael L. Gibler. Coffman then supervised the evacuation of several dozen wounded commandos. Still refusing evacuation, he then led a squad-size element to the 4-West Iraqi police station to make contact with the surviving commandos there. Once the station was secure, the Strykers of 3-21st Infantry pushed on to clear the immediate area of all insurgents. Coffman ultimately returned to his original position to ensure the evacuation of all of the Iraqi casualties; only then did he consent to evacuation for surgery for his own serious wound.[7]

In the fight for the 4-West police station, 12 Iraqi commandos were killed. Most of the 48 wounded were evacuated to Forward Operating Base Freedom on the west side of the river, and the 10 seriously wounded were taken to the Army's 37th Combat Support Hosptial at Mosul airfield. Later, the less seriously wounded were moved to Mosul General Hospital. Although the number of insurgents was unknown, many locals said there were at least 100 wounded in addition to the 25 confirmed killed.

For his actions in Mosul, Coffman received the Distinguished Service Cross in a ceremony in Baghdad's Adnon Palace on 24 August 2005. Iraq's Minister of Interior, Bayan Jabr, and Thavit were on hand to present Iraqi medallions. "Colonel Coffman, the blood you shed will never be forgotten," said Jabr. "We, the forces of the Ministry of Interior and the Ministry of Defense will continue to fight until we defeat terrorism. Right will always defeat wrong." In response, Coffman addressed his commando comrades: "Third Battalion, I am truly, truly honored to stand here with you today and remember your courage and bravery last November and in all the days since then. It has been an honor to fight with you." Coffman praised the commandos for their service and commitment to defending freedom in Iraq. He said he viewed the ceremony as a tribute to the Iraqi and Coalition forces that had fought, bled, and died together. "I'm very proud of them, and more importantly, they're proud of themselves," Coffman said. "The next day, they were back out on patrol—after suffering 30 to 50 percent casualties. That's pretty amazing. I'm not sure American units would do that. That says something about their resilience and their ability to maintain morale. They certainly mourned their losses, but they got back into the fight right away. I don't think you can ask much more of people than that."[8]

In the months following the battle in Mosul, Coffman refused to see himself as a hero, just a Soldier who did what he had to do to keep himself and his comrades alive. His wound was a constant reminder of that day. Surgery repaired the shattered bones in his hand, but he would never be whole again. In Coffman's own words, "The wounds have healed, but I do not have full dexterity in my left hand. I would rate it at about 90 percent."[9]

The desperate fight of the Iraqi commandos was not in vain. Mosul was secured in November 2004 and the insurgency greatly weakened. During the pivotal January 2005 elections, the commandos were instrumental in protecting the polling sites and ensuring the overall success of the election process. Voter participation reached more than 80 percent in Mosul. A permanent Iraqi government emerged, ending the era of the provisional structure. The gallant efforts of Coffman and the Iraqi commandos helped make this all possible.

*   *   *

Coffman's fight is a classic study of leadership in a crisis situation. By keeping his composure and applying the combat skills learned over a long career, Coffman staved off disaster for himself and his comrades. As an advisor, he was not in the Iraqi chain of command nor was he expected to participate in direct combat. When the Iraqi officers were incapacitated by enemy fire, Coffman jumped into the leadership void, overcame a significant language barrier and wounds, and motivated the surviving commandos by his personal actions. Instead of undermining unit cohesion and morale, he strengthened it and organized a successful defense against almost impossible odds.

The training and materiel support given by Coffman and sanctioned by the MNSTC-I were instrumental in the success of the commandos on 14 November. The weapons, equipment, and the training to use them were apparent, and the transport provided by the Coalition facilitated their rapid response to the troubled city. Capable of conducting coordinated multinational operations, the commandos proved themselves to be a reliable ally in the fight against the insurgents. They were a highly disciplined force in comparison with other Iraqi units. Remarkably, the surviving commandos were back on the streets the next day after suffering heavy casualties and the trauma of prolonged and intense combat.

The actions of the commandos had further ramifications than the casualties inflicted on the insurgency. They tied down a significant number of insurgents, which would have been free to cause further harm and mischief in other areas of the city and thwart the efforts of the American 1st Brigade in clearing their sectors. The commandos served as a shining example for the Iraqi people and gave legitimacy to the interim government. Finally, by weakening the insurgency in November and subsequent security operations, the commandos were instrumental in the successful elections the following January.

Notes

1.   Much of the information presented in this case study came from media reports and the citation for COL Coffman's award for valor. Coffman and LTC Gibler, commanding 3d Battalion, 21st Infantry Regiment, contributed significantly through e-mail correspondence with the author, filling in gaps, and making corrections. No classified information was considered or used as source material.

2.   Matt Murphy, "Iraqi Police Commandos Lead the Way" *Defend America News,* 16 February 2005, online at <http://www.defendamerica.mil/articles/feb2005/a0216051a1.html>, accessed 25 May 2006. Anthony H. Cordesman and Arleigh A. Burke, *Iraqi Force Development: Testimony Before the Subcommittee on National Security, Emerging Threats, and International Relations Committee on Government Reform, United States House of Representatives* (Washington, DC: Center for Strategic and International Studies, 14 March 2005), 15–16.

3.   The 1st Brigade consisted of the 1-5, 3-21, and 1-24 Infantry Battalions, as well as the 2d Squadron, 14th Cavalry Squadron and 2d Battalion, 8th Field Artillery.

4.   Jim Steele was later awarded the Special Forces Gold Medal by the government of Iraq for his heroic efforts in this operation.

5.   Media reports say "all but one officer" were wounded or killed. Coffman indicated all of the commando officers were down and the media was mistaken. They unintentionally confused the term "officer" referring to a commissioned officer with that of a police officer.

6.   Joe Kane, "MNSTC-I Advisor Fights Beside Iraqi Commandos," *The Advisor*, Volume 1 Issue 11, 20 November 2004, online at <http://www.mnstci.iraq.centcom.mil//docs/advisor/archive/112004/20NovThe Advisor.pdf>, accessed 25 May 2006, 4, 7.

7.   The 3-21's area of operations was the east side of the Tigris River. Elements of this unit crossed into the 1-24 sector to aid the commandos. Gibler personally led Company C along with his forward command element into the fray.

8.   Joseph Chenelly, "Colonel Awarded Distinguished Service Cross for Rallying Iraqi Troops in Mosul Fighting" *Army Times*, 26 August 2005, online at <http://www.armytimes.com/story.php?f=1-292925-1060306.php>, accessed 25 May 2006. The Distinguished Service Cross is second only to the Medal of Honor in military decorations.

9.   Two joints were shattered in Coffman's left hand.

Action at Combat Outpost Tampa
Mosul, 29 December 2004

by

John J. McGrath

I remember hearing that Mosul was the next Fallujah and thinking, yeah, it already is.

—1LT Sean Keneally, Platoon Leader,
C Company, 1-24th Infantry, 2004[1]

Counterinsurgency operations are generally offensive in nature. Forces conducting such operations typically seek out and battle the insurgents where they are most active. However, counterinsurgency also involves the protection of the local population and the force itself. This is usually accomplished by the establishment of permanent or semipermanent fortified outposts in areas of extensive insurgent activity. The creation of such positions can place the counterinsurgent forces into a reactive posture. The insurgents may find such outposts to be too ripe a target to ignore and mass forces in an attempt to destroy the garrison. Sophisticated insurgent planners and forces may also coordinate their attack on the fixed location with an ambush against counterinsurgent forces responding to the initial attack. Just such an operation was mounted against elements of the 1st Battalion, 24th Infantry, on 29 December 2004, at a position called Combat Outpost (COP) Tampa, in western Mosul, Iraq. The reaction of American forces to this well-coordinated insurgent attack is the focus of this case study.

Mosul is the third-largest city in Iraq and the capital of the northern province of Nineveh. It was established in the early Islamic period on the west bank of the Tigris River, opposite the ruins of Nineveh, the capital of the ancient Assyrian Empire. It was an important trading center on the main caravan trade route between India and Persia and the Mediterranean before the completion of the Suez Canal in the 19th century. In the 20th century, it became a gateway to the oil fields discovered northeast of the city. Mosul then grew up on both sides of the Tigris and by 2003, with an estimated population of 1.7 million, was the third-largest city in Iraq (after Baghdad and Basra) and the largest city in the northern third of the country.[2] The city was a melting pot, with large Kurdish, Christian (Assyrians and Chaldeans), and Turkmen minorities. By 2004, Sunni Arabs had majority status in the city, the result of a combination of factors including a Baathist Arabization resettlement policy commencing in the 1970s. The portion of Mosul west of the Tigris River was predominately Sunni Arab, while the portion east of the river contained most of the Kurdish population. Thus, the city represents all the ethnic challenges in a microcosm facing a post-Baathist Iraq.[3]

The portion of Mosul west of the Tigris River consisted of the oldest and poorest sections, and included several neighborhoods considered hotbeds of Sunni insurgent activities. The densely populated older section of western Mosul, next to the Tigris River, had narrow streets and closely packed buildings. This area also contained government buildings for both the city and province. Newer districts, extending to the north, south, and west of the old city, while still urban, also had a mix of industrial and residential areas with wider streets that better facilitated the maneuver of military vehicles.[4] Iraqi National Route 1, a divided highway, also known to the US forces as Main Supply Route (MSR) TAMPA, ran in a north-south direction through Mosul to the west of the old city. A number of key roads, including MSR TAMPA, intersected at the Yarmuk Traffic Circle northwest of the old city. The neighborhoods around this important intersection were the areas of most intense insurgent activity in late 2004. There were several key east-west routes running through western Mosul as well. Route BARRACUDA was a major thoroughfare that intersected MSR TAMPA several blocks south of Yarmuk Circle. Several blocks south of BARRACUDA was Route NISSAN which also intersected MSR TAMPA and ran eastward through the northern portion of the old city and across the Tigris River across the fourth bridge (counting from the south). BARRACUDA ran into NISSAN about a kilometer and a half east of MSR TAMPA. In the southwestern corner of the city, Routes (north to south) LEXUS and HONDA ran eastward from MSR TAMPA, joining at a large traffic circle to become Route SAAB. SAAB ran through the old city crossing the Tigris over the first bridge.

Key installations in western Mosul included the government building called Provincial Hall and three police stations. These stations were 1-West, located several blocks west of Provincial Hall; 3-West, located northwest of the old city, east of MSR TAMPA, and north of Route NISSAN; and 4-West, located on MSR TAMPA northwest of the Yarmuk Circle between the circle and the first bridge, where MSR TAMPA crossed the Tigris.

Three miles from the old city, on the southwestern edge of Mosul, was the large municipal airport. On arrival in Mosul, US forces transformed the airport and an adjacent Iraqi military compound called Camp Ghazlani into a large base camp complex and rechristened the airbase Logistics Support Area (LSA) Diamondback. The former Iraqi military complex had several different names, ultimately being called Forward Operating Base (FOB) Marez.[5] Marez, located on a hill overlooking Mosul from the south, had a long history as an Iraqi military installation. During the British mandate, the post was known as Tank Hill Camp. In the Baathist era, a portion of the camp, known as Salammiyah Camp, had been the headquarters of the Iraqi 5th Corps, which had commanded all Iraqi army forces in northern Iraq. These two base camps would become the main cantonment for the US forces operating in western Mosul (and, in some cases, elsewhere in the Nineveh province) and the main logistics hub for the whole multinational force in northwestern Iraq.

Mosul was not directly involved in the major combat operations of March and April 2003. On 11 April, the Iraqi 5th Corps surrendered to a joint Kurdish-American force. A small force of Marines then arrived in the city and set up a base at the airport. The first substantial American presence in the city was the deployment of a brigade of the 101st Airborne Division (Air Assault) on 20 April 2003, followed by the bulk of the division within a few days.[6] While Mosul went through the various troop rotations of Operation IRAQI FREEDOM (OIF) from 2003 to 2004, the city also went through several cycles of turmoil and stability. Initially, during the OIF-I deployment, under the 101st Airborne Division, the city was fairly calm except for the firefight which resulted in the deaths of Uday and Qusay Hussein in July 2003. This stability continued in the OIF-II deployment, even though the 101st was replaced in early 2004 in Nineveh province by only a brigade-sized force—the 3d Brigade, 2d Infantry Division, from Fort Lewis, Washington.[7] The 3d Brigade was the Army's first unit equipped with the Stryker wheeled armored combat vehicle.

At the end of the OIF-II deployment, insurgent-initiated violence in Mosul increased greatly. This roughly coincided with the I Marine Expeditionary Force's joint assault on the city of Fallujah in Anbar province in November 2004. Sunni insurgents had seemingly massed in the Mosul metropolis in response to the pressure at Fallujah or to provide a diversion from operations in the south. The higher intensity of insurgent operations could also have been a concentrated effort to disrupt the January 2005 Iraqi constitutional assembly elections.[8] For the third troop rotation of Operation IRAQI FREEDOM in Mosul, the US Army replaced the 3d Brigade, 2d Infantry Division, with a similarly organized unit, the 1st Brigade, 25th Infantry Division, out of Fort Lewis, Washington. The 1st Battalion, 24th Infantry (1-24), unofficially nicknamed Deuce Four, a Stryker infantry unit, was given responsibility for the western half of Mosul. The battalion was operational by the end of October 2004.[9]

The members of 1-24 had minimal combat experience prior to arrival in Mosul. The battalion had been stationed at Fort Lewis since 1991, receiving its current designation in August 1995.[10] In October 1999, then Army Chief of Staff General Eric Shinseki announced the transformation of two light infantry brigades stationed at Fort Lewis into one medium brigade equipped with a yet-to-be-fielded armored wheeled vehicle.[11] One of these brigades was the 1-24's parent unit, the 1st Brigade, 25th Infantry Division. The wheeled vehicle was developed and later named the Stryker after two Army Medal of Honor winners. The brigade had been slated to become the second Stryker unit and, starting in the spring of 2002, had converted from a light infantry configuration to the new Stryker brigade organization.

The Stryker was designed to provide a solution to the mobility and survivability weaknesses of light infantry and the deployability problems of mechanized infantry and armor units in one package. It was an eight-wheeled armored vehicle, which came in various configurations such as infantry carrier, reconnaissance, command, medical, and signal. Together all the variants weighed less than 19 tons, easing air deployment concerns. Most variants were equipped with a turret-mounted .50-caliber machine gun or MK19 automatic grenade launcher.[12] Modern digital communications and information packages were an integral part of the Stryker system.[13] One variant of the Stryker, the mobile gun system (MGS), was not yet fielded. The MGS Strykers were equipped with the tube-launched, optically tracked, wire-guided (TOW) antiarmor missile system. To combat the extensive insurgent use of the shaped charges fired from rocket propelled grenade (RPG) weapons against American vehicles, Strykers deployed to Iraq were retrofitted with an external wire skirt. The development and deployment of the Strykers was considered controversial, but the vehicle proved to be effective in the urban environment.[14]

Despite having few combat veterans in the unit, 1-24 was relatively well prepared for its yearlong deployment to Mosul. The battalion had trained extensively for the mission. This training included participation in a highly successful rotation at the Army's Joint Readiness Training Center (JRTC) at Fort Polk, Louisiana, and the completion of a training regimen that included complicated platoon live-fire exercises and leader development instruction that emphasized civil affairs aspects of counter-insurgency warfare.[15] Experienced officers led the Soldiers of the 1-24. The battalion commander, LTC Michael Erik Kurilla, a 1988 US Military Academy graduate, was an experienced infantry officer who had served in the 1989 invasion of Panama, DESERT STORM, Haiti, Bosnia, and

Kosovo, and had commanded the battalion for 5 months before it deployed to Mosul. His key subordinates were similarly experienced officers and included executive officer (XO) MAJ Michael Lawrence, who would primarily run the battalion's base at FOB Marez, operations officer (S3) MAJ Mark Bieger, who would spend most days out in the city coordinating and fine-tuning operations, and CSM Robert Prosser. As of 29 December 2004, with one exception, the company commanders had been in their positions prior to deployment and included CPT Jeffrey Vanantwerp (A), CPT Bryan Carroll (B), CPT Christopher Hossfeld (C), and CPT Matthew McGrew (HHC).[16]

Deuce Four was organized under the Stryker battalion structure, which consisted of a headquarters and headquarters company (1-24 referred to it as Hatchet) and three infantry (or line) companies, A or Apache, B or Bulldog, and C or Cobra. Each line company contained 21 Stryker vehicles and was organized into 3 infantry platoons, a mobile gun system platoon, a mortar section, and a company headquarters. Each infantry platoon had four infantry Strykers. The MGS platoon was equipped with three Strykers armed with TOW antiarmor missile systems. The mortar section had two Stryker-mounted 120-mm mortars. The company headquarters consisted of two command Strykers, an ambulance Stryker, a fire support Stryker, and a three-man sniper team. At the battalion level, the headquarters company contained a reconnaissance platoon (referred to as Hunter), a mortar platoon with four 120-mm mortars, a medical platoon, and a seven-man sniper squad. The battalion headquarters itself had assigned Strykers for the use of the battalion commander and operations officer (S3) and several additional vehicles with specialized communications equipment. Hunter platoon consisted of four Strykers, with three five-Soldier reconnaissance teams. Almost every Stryker in the battalion had an assigned crew consisting of a driver and a vehicle commander, the latter usually being a sergeant (E5). This account focuses on the activities of Cobra Company, the battalion tactical command group (BN TAC), and the battalion reconnaissance platoon, the major participants in the actions on 29 December 2004.[17]

By the end of October, 1-24 was in place in western Mosul. This routine rotational turnover between OIF-II and OIF-III units coincided with a period of increased activity in Mosul. November 2004 would prove to be the most intense period of combat activity in Mosul so far during OIF. In the months before the arrival of 1-24 in Mosul, the enemy usage of improvised explosive devices (IEDs) and vehicle-borne IEDs (VBIEDs) had increased in the city, along with the number of direct-fire contacts with the Anti-Iraqi Forces (AIF). Many of these contacts were the result of proactive patrols seeking out the cells emplacing IEDs. Because of defeats at the hands of US forces, the AIF had started to direct its efforts against the Iraqi Security Forces (ISF) in Mosul and were mounting larger and more coordinated attacks against the local Iraqi forces. These trends continued with the arrival of Deuce Four.[18]

The 1-24 was first bombarded with mortar shells. When patrols took out the mortar crews, the insurgents began attacking Iraqi civilians. This followed with attempts to gain de facto control of portions of the city. The large-scale attack on 10 November was the start of this. This attack, aimed at local police and Iraqi National Guard forces, soon virtually destroyed Iraqi civil authority and law enforcement capabilities. In western Mosul, the insurgents quickly overran four of the five police stations, all but the main police headquarters, with some 3,200 of the 4,000 mostly Sunni Arab policemen abandoning their posts and fleeing. The AIF ransacked the stations, taking or destroying anything of value and usually then abandoning the station. ISF patrols were ambushed as well, although the focus of the enemy attacks was on the fixed locations of the police stations. The insurgents followed up this success with a series of large-scale attacks and efforts to control whole Mosul neighborhoods. Over the next few weeks, there was a terror campaign designed to intimidate the local population prior to the January 2005 elections.[19]

The 1-24 was quickly committed to this fight. By midday on 11 November, the Iraqi provincial governor asked for American assistance. The Deuce Four had already been conducting operations along MSR TAMPA. What started as a small raid along the MSR turned into a major clearing operation, the first battle of Yarmuk Circle, when the massed insurgents fought back. The insurgents controlled MSR TAMPA from Route BARRACUDA north to the circle. Apache Company, supported by other battalion elements, primarily Bulldog, was in a 6-hour firefight with a force of over 60 AIF members that ended in the destruction of the insurgent force at the cost of one Apache trooper killed in action (KIA), the battalion's first fatality in Iraq.[20] On 14 November, a force composed of Iraqi police commandos, elements of the neighboring Stryker battalion (3-21st Infantry), and a Deuce Four Apache Company quick reaction force (QRF) platoon repelled an insurgent attack on the 4-West police station in the northern portion of western Mosul. The retaking of 4-West marked the return of control of all Mosul police stations to Coalition forces.[21]

While the insurgents did not retain permanent possession of any part of Mosul, their intense campaign to disrupt the January elections continued into December. The AIF hoped to create an unsafe environment for voters with head-to-head firefights and large ambushes. Almost every US patrol would make contact several times every day. Soon, contacts had risen from 3 or 4 a day 6 months earlier to 25 to 35 a day.[22] On 13 December, AIF elements were again astride MSR TAMPA south of Yarmuk Circle, extending below Route NISSAN. In this second battle of Yarmuk Circle, Cobra Company attacked northward, once again clearing the road up to the circle.[23] The culmination of these large battles in December would be the action at Combat Outpost Tampa on 29 December. However, the AIF had other weapons in their arsenal. The most significant enemy attack in December took place on FOB Marez on 21 December when a suicide attacker detonated a bomb inside the main dining facility killing 22 Soldiers, including Apache Company Commander CPT William Jacobsen. This setback clearly illustrated the difficulty in detecting terrorists, who could hide even among post support workers, and the dangerous capabilities the enemy possessed.

The insurgent, or Anti-Iraqi Forces, in the Mosul area in 2004 and 2005 consisted of six distinct groups. Five of these were groups of Islamic extremists, each with slightly different goals and beliefs.[24] One of these groups claimed affiliation with al-Qaeda. All these elements were fanatical in their commitment to the cause and usually worked together for the common goal. Apart from these religious radicals, there was also a group of former regime elements (FRE), somewhat less fanatical Sunni Baathists, operating to destabilize the new government. Accordingly, the FRE primarily targeted the representatives of the new Iraqi government. The FRE and extremists only worked in concert when they had to, otherwise being at odds with each other.[25] Estimates for the size of insurgent forces in Mosul were between 400 to 500 active members, supported by 2,000 to 2,500 part-time or intermittent elements. While these forces were fragmented, and the FRE forces were at odds with the rest, the AIF did seem able to coordinate operations occasionally, particularly during the pre-election offensive in November 2004.

The most sophisticated of these groups was Abu Musab al-Zarqawi's al-Qaeda in Mesopotamia. The importance that Zarqawi placed on Mosul was evident by his appointment of a Mosul resident, Mohammed Khalid Sharkawa (also spelled Shaiker and known by the alias Abu Talha) as his chief deputy. Sharkawa was responsible for all al-Qaeda operations in Iraq north of the Euphrates River. Prior to 29 December, Sharkawa had claimed responsibility for numerous terror attacks against Mosul civilians and ISF personnel.[26] Sharkawa worked in the background. The intertwining of the Islamic extremist groups can be seen in descriptions of Sharkawa's position. Some sources claimed he was a leader of the *Ansar al-Summah* Army, the group that claimed credit for the 21 December mess hall bombing. Despite being from the insurgent hotbed town of Qabr Abed south of Mosul, Sharkawa converted to extremist Islamic beliefs only after a career as an officer in the Baathist Republican Guard and as a smuggler. US intelligence had earlier considered him a criminal rather than a terrorist. Sharkawa reputedly met directly with Zarqawi on a monthly basis outside of Mosul. By the end of December, after almost 2 months of devastating losses, the insurgent leadership planned a big strike to regain the initiative. The elections were still a month away and it seemed that their tenuous grip on the Sunni population of western Mosul was slipping away. Sharkawa and his colleagues decided to try one more large operation in western Mosul, one designed to destroy or grievously wound the American forces garrisoning and patrolling in the center of their western Mosul stronghold.[27]

In the heightened security and intensive operations before the election, the 1-24 was responsible for an area of operations (AO) that consisted of about 800 square kilometers (497 square miles), and included all of Mosul west of the Tigris River. The AO also encompassed a large expanse of virtually uninhabited desert, plus about a dozen small towns west of the city. These areas outside the city, where enemy activity was usually nonexistent, were managed on an economy of force basis as necessary at the battalion level. The bulk of Deuce Four combat power remained in the city. In essence, the battalion's mission was to find, fix, and destroy all noncompliant forces in its AO. Each of the three companies was assigned its own AO within the battalion sector, all in western Mosul. Apache Company drew the densely populated old city area and the cluster of government buildings, while Bulldog Company had a sector of northwest Mosul. Cobra Company, the focus of this study, had responsibility for the western portion of the city from the edge of the old city to the western outskirts. MSR TAMPA ran through the middle of Cobra Company's sector.[28]

The battalion Reconnaissance (Recon) Platoon usually provided security for the battalion commander's tactical command post (TAC), which moved throughout the battalion AO on a daily basis. Additional TACs were organized at company level. These forces were primarily command and control elements, but they also possessed extensive firepower in their assigned Strykers. This made the TAC, supported by the Recon Platoon, into a separate maneuver element in its own right in addition to a command and control element. The same was true for the company TAC elements.

In December 2004, the Deuce Four battle rhythm consisted of a complex series of interlocking daily operations designed to restore security to the residents of Mosul, assist in the development of the ISF and police, and develop intelligence. The battalion averaged about 30 combat patrols and 4 raids daily. Platoons (infantry and MGS) would typically execute one patrol in the early morning and a second in the early evening, averaging about 8 hours of combat patrolling per day. Raids were generally conducted at night, based on fresh intelligence information, and averaged between two to four operations a week. The battalion and company commanders participated in patrols either with a specific platoon or as an independent TAC element, spending a similar amount of time in the city, as did the patrolling platoons. Commanders at all levels were expected to meet local leaders, officials, and business leaders on a daily basis. The large cantonment and logistics base, FOB Marez and the adjacent LSA Diamondback, also included the support elements of the 1-24's parent brigade and various other units. Except when manning combat outposts or temporary FOBs in the city, Deuce Four units were garrisoned at Marez and, therefore, were also partially responsible for the post's security. This included the periodic rotation of 1-24 platoons through the defensive perimeter. Additionally, the battalion retained a platoon daily at Marez as a quick reaction force (QRF) prepared to move anywhere within the battalion sector at a minute's notice.[29]

After the collapse of civil authority in western Mosul, Kurilla decided there was a need to retain a permanent presence at key points within Mosul. Accordingly, each company established platoon-size combat outposts within their company AOs. Apache established a full-time presence at the Provincial Hall and at the 1-West police station, both in the old city section of Mosul. Bulldog placed a garrison at the scene of the battle on 14 November, the 4-West police station on MSR TAMPA, northwest of Yarmuk Circle. In its sector, Cobra initially placed a garrison at the 3-West police station. Platoons rotated every day between outpost duty and patrol duty. Outpost duty lasted about 20 hours. Because of the strain on the platoons, the company headquarters took turns at patrolling to allow the platoons to rest between missions. The recurring conflict along the portion of MSR TAMPA south of Yarmuk Circle emphasized the need for a permanent presence along that route. To fulfill this need, Cobra established COP Tampa in mid-December, south of Route NISSAN on MSR TAMPA in the heart of the Mosul neighborhood considered the insurgents' stronghold.[30]

The second battle of Yarmuk Circle on 13 December was the event that established the need for a new combat outpost. This was the second sizable battle along the stretch of MSR TAMPA south of Yarmuk Circle in a month. Cobra Company Commander Hossfeld conducted a reconnaissance of the area on 18 December and selected a four-story concrete building on the east side of MSR TAMPA at a crossroads several blocks south of the intersection of MSR TAMPA and Route NISSAN. US troops had damaged the building, previously used by the AIF, several weeks earlier. As a result, the structure, formerly containing shops on the first floor and apartments on the upper floors, was unoccupied except for the presence of a family of Iraqi squatters living in one of the third floor apartments. After paying the squatters $500 to leave, Cobra's 2d Platoon established the outpost on 20 December.[31] The height of the building, which towered over its neighbors, allowed observers on the upper floors and the roof to overlook the entire area south of Yarmuk Circle in all directions. That put the COP Tampa garrison in a key position to observe all activity in the heartland of the Sunni insurgency in Mosul.[32]

After the establishment of COP Tampa, 1-24 continued its rigorous patrolling, while occupying five outposts in the city. The terror campaign against Iraqi civilians and soldiers continued, as well as IED and RPG firings at US vehicles. On 28 December, the bodies of seven Iraqi National Guard soldiers were found just outside LSA Diamondback. On that same day, 1-24 conducted a cordon and search operation and detained 15 people for planning and conducting insurgent activities. The 1-24 caught an additional three IED bomb suspects after a chase.[33] Such operations often produced intelligence.

On 28 December, Deuce Four leaders received information that 15 suicide bombers in the Mosul area had just completed training and their masters intended to use them to conduct a major attack on one of the American outposts in western Mosul. A previous intelligence memo had mentioned that two large trucks, capable of carrying a large amount of explosive materials, had been sent to the city for use as VBIEDs. The most likely targets for such attacks were three US outposts positioned deep within an area of intensive insurgent activity in Mosul: the 3-West and 4-West police stations and COP Tampa. Of the three, COP Tampa's defenses were the only ones not previously tested by the AIF. COP Tampa was also the outpost deepest within the main AIF operational area.[34]

Kurilla and his company commanders faced the decision of how best to respond to the intelligence of a pending attack. With the mess hall massacre still a recent memory and the elections just a month away, it seemed likely the AIF would mount at least one major operation in the city designed to disrupt the vote. Therefore, the 1-24 could not ignore any intelligence of threats. The choices available to the 1-24 leadership included the following: do nothing; reinforce the combat outpost garrisons with additional troops; reinforce the defenses of the outposts without reinforcing the garrisons; and withdraw the garrisons to FOB Marez until the threat passed and outside reinforcements had arrived. Each of these choices had their advantages and disadvantages.

To do nothing would mean that the 1-24 leadership believed the current arrangements were already adequate. However, such inaction could lead to a critical underestimation of the enemy. Undoubtedly, the AIF had seen and analyzed the US defenses and patrol patterns and had developed techniques to defeat them in their current configurations. Reinforcing the combat outpost garrisons with additional troops was a double-edged sword. The larger garrisons would bring additional firepower and possibly, by their mere size, deter attacks. Because of their static nature, however, such positions could also provide the enemy with a larger target to attack. Moreover, at least in the short term, larger garrisons would have to be taken from the forces already available. Units formerly committed to patrolling, quick reaction, and immediate response to intelligence information would instead be committed to static defensive positions. While these posts could prove to be quite formidable, the enemy would now have the initiative. Even without attacking any fixed points, the lack of counterinsurgent forces patrolling and raiding throughout the city would cede tacit control of large areas to the insurgents. Also, if the insurgents did assemble a large enough force to attack an outpost, there would be no troops available to reinforce or relieve beleaguered garrisons.

Reinforcing the outposts with increased fortifications and firepower was an option that could be implemented quickly. Furthermore, this action could force the enemy to delay an attack to adjust to the additional fortifications. Such a delay could provide time for expected reinforcements to arrive at Mosul. This course of action would also retain the maximum number of patrolling and reaction forces. However, it was difficult to judge how much increased fortification would be necessary, particularly at COP Tampa, which had not yet come under enemy attack, but was located along a major highway that permitted enemy forces to approach at high speed. Withdrawing all the garrisons to Marez and depending solely on extensive patrolling to control western Mosul, at least until expected reinforcements arrived in a few weeks, would provide the maximum force protection for US troops. Even so, it would also be observed by both the enemy and civil population as a de facto defeat for American forces, possibly emboldening the enemy. (See map 4.)

*   *   *

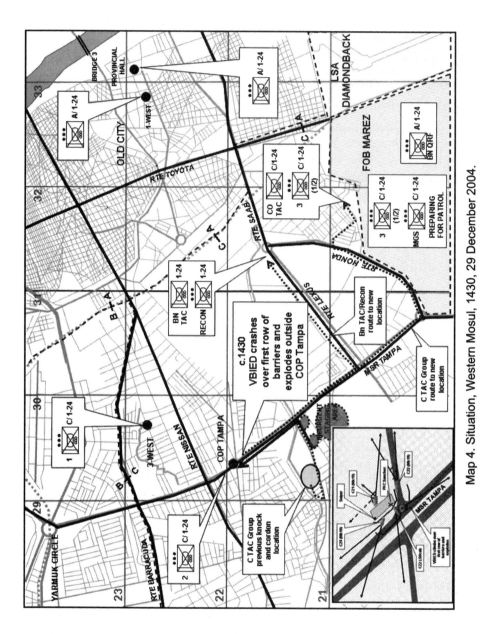

Map 4. Situation, Western Mosul, 1430, 29 December 2004.

Kurilla decided to reinforce the defenses of the combat outposts in response to the intelligence information. Accordingly, Cobra Company Commander Hossfeld immediately set out to provide COP Tampa with an extra set of barriers and an additional heavy machine gun. In the early morning hours of 29 December, under the cover of darkness, engineer troops emplaced a second row of barriers at COP Tampa along the MSR, extending out to the rightmost, northbound, lane of that four-lane boulevard. This move provided two sets of barriers in front of the COP along the most likely approach route for a VBIED. The new row pushed the COP perimeter almost 100 feet farther away from the building. If the first row did not stop a suicide bomber, it was believed the second row surely would.[35]

Later that same morning, 2d Platoon, C Company, 1-24th Infantry, led by 1LT Jeremy Rockwell and SFC Mark Gallegos, rotated back into garrison duty at COP Tampa, the post it had established 9 days earlier. The platoon placed its four Strykers around the perimeter of the outpost. Two vehicles were placed along MSR TAMPA, one facing north and the other south, behind the two rows of barriers on the western side along the MSR. On the eastern side of the outpost, the other two Strykers covered the roads approaching COP Tampa from that direction. The 2d Platoon, with about 40 Soldiers, manned positions either in the Strykers or in windows on the building's third floor. Each squad manned two positions at a time for a total of six positions overall. Guard shifts were 1 hour on and 2 hours off. Off-duty Soldiers usually tried to sleep on the second floor. Hossfeld attached a company sniper to the platoon, SGT Daniel Schwendeman. Schwendeman positioned himself on the roof of the building in the northwest corner where he could observe activity in the general direction of Yarmuk Circle. Schwendeman originally had planned to occupy one of the buildings on the opposite side of MSR TAMPA from the COP, but there were no positions elsewhere as good as the rooftop of the COP itself.[36]

At about 1430, PFC Oscar Sanchez was on guard duty in a window in the southwestern part of the building. Sanchez' view faced south along MSR TAMPA. For better visibility, Sanchez stood on a chair. He was armed with an M240 7.62-mm machine gun. Minutes before, the battalion TAC/Recon group had departed the COP to go to the Apache Company outpost at Provincial Hall. The TAC/Recon group consisted of six Strykers, including the battalion command group (Kurilla and Prosser) and the S3 (Bieger) and the battalion Recon Platoon. This force had proceeded south on MSR TAMPA to Route LEXUS and was approaching the junction of Routes HONDA and LEXUS. About 500 meters southeast of the TAC/Recon group, Hossfeld was moving in a southwestern Mosul neighborhood, preparing to conduct what Cobra informally called a cordon and knock operation with his tactical command post and part of the company's 3d Platoon. This C TAC group consisted of four Strykers. In a cordon and knock operation, the unit surrounding a neighborhood and dismounted Soldiers went door-to-door interviewing the local residents while searching houses for ammunition and weapons. The C TAC group, like the battalion TAC/Recon group, had just been to the northeast of its current location, near COP Tampa. Hossfeld's force had completed a cordon and knock operation in a neighborhood west of MSR TAMPA, about 1,000 meters southwest of COP Tampa.[37]

En route to the new location, Hossfeld had noticed a dump truck parked beside a road leading to MSR TAMPA. While the truck was somewhat out of place, the area included several vehicular maintenance shops and could have had a legitimate reason for being there. What the Cobra commander did not know was that the truck was loaded with about 50 South African-made 155-mm artillery shells and propane tanks. The driver, a suicide bomber, was just waiting for the order to execute his mission: an assault on COP Tampa. After Hossfeld's group departed the area, the truck waited for the battalion TAC/Recon group to pass by to the south on MSR TAMPA. After it passed, the truck driver pulled up to the MSR, got out of the vehicle, and made a final statement to a video camera carried by his superiors to film the attack. Then, at about 1430, the driver climbed back into the vehicle, crossed over MSR TAMPA to the northbound lanes, and sped toward the combat outpost.[38]

As the dump truck moved along the MSR, on the roof of COP Tampa sniper Schwendeman and platoon leader Rockwell were looking in the opposite direction. However, they sensed something was amiss as the usual flow of traffic on MSR TAMPA had suddenly stopped. On the third floor, Sanchez saw the truck's approach. The truck's tires had been overinflated to best use its momentum from traveling up MSR TAMPA to get over the barriers in front of the combat outpost and strike the building directly. As the vehicle approached the barriers, which restricted northbound traffic on MSR TAMPA to one lane, the driver veered to the right and drove the dump truck over the first row of barriers. Sanchez immediately fired on the vehicle, whose driver was now facing an unexpected second set of barriers. The explosives detonated. The massive blast critically wounded Sanchez. However, since the vehicle detonated about 75 feet from the building, it did not annihilate the outpost. The explosion created a large crater 15 feet in length and 4 feet deep in front of the building. On the roof, Rockwell and Schwendeman were blown diagonally across to the southeast corner. Inside the building and in the nearby Strykers, 11 2d Platoon Soldiers, in addition to Sanchez, were wounded. The external façade of the building was greatly damaged. The two Strykers facing the explosion were also damaged. The one closest to impact caught on fire when the onboard supply of white phosphorus, used to create a smoke screen, ignited. Despite their proximity to the explosion, no Soldiers were killed in the Strykers.

The driver of the nearest Styker, PFC Harland Leaverton, was critically wounded, but survived because he was napping in the driver's seat and not sitting up when the VBIED went off. PFC Faustino Nava, the driver of the other nearby vehicle, suffered a leg injury. Nava was not in the hatch when the VBIED struck, but was climbing into the vehicle and protected by its armor. However, shrapnel temporarily blinded his vehicle commander.[39]

According to many observers, the explosion was the largest heard during their time in Mosul. The cloud of smoke was clearly visible throughout the city. Most personnel initially thought something had happened at or near Yarmuk Circle, but a radio message on the battalion frequency from 2d Platoon's Gallegos soon indicated otherwise. Gallegos reported two critical casualties and a plea for reinforcements. After his message, communications with the COP were temporarily lost as the defenders were now involved in a furious firefight. A force of roughly 50 AIF fighters, armed with RPGs and small arms, immediately opened fire on the COP garrison, shooting at the defenders from neighboring rooftops and street corners to the north, west, and east. This was the beginning of what proved to be a 2-hour firefight. (See map 5.) The enemy fire forced the garrison to remain inside the COP building once casualties were evacuated from the Strykers. When the platoon began to run low on ammunition, individual Soldiers braved the AIF fire to retrieve ammunition stored in the damaged Strykers.[40]

The two nearest reinforcements to COP Tampa when Gallegos' message was received were the battalion TAC/Recon group and the C TAC group. The TAC/Recon group was more than halfway along the 2-mile route from COP Tampa to the Apache Company COP at Provincial Hall when the explosion reverberated in the distance. This force was on Route LEXUS, a broad thoroughfare that enabled it to turn around immediately. The C TAC group was located to the south on a narrower street. Both commanders heard the call from Gallegos and the subsequent loss of contact. The situation at COP Tampa seemed critical and the leaders of each group, battalion commander Kurilla and company commander Hossfeld, were faced with decisions involving how to respond to the situation.

These commanders had several immediate options. As command and control nodes, they could move to a forward position, direct the reinforcement of the outpost, and coordinate the dispatch of the quick reaction force, other reinforcements, and medical evacuation teams. This choice left the commanders free to coordinate the activities of the remainder of their units while organizing a relief force for COP Tampa. Neither commander knew whether the attack on the outpost was a prelude to further attacks on other battalion and company elements in similar forward positions. This choice would allow the commanders to command their units without themselves having to fight at the same time.

A second option was to organize the relief while "moving to the sound of the guns." This choice offered the advantage of bringing forward the immediate firepower of the Strykers and the Soldiers in each group. The TAC/Recon group, aside from consisting of the battalion tactical command post, also included the battalion Recon Platoon with its four Strykers, three reconnaissance teams, and a sniper team. The C TAC group similarly included the two vehicles of the company tactical command post plus two Strykers and one squad from Cobra's 3d Platoon. By providing immediate reinforcement, not only could the two groups bring instantaneous support and firepower, they could also provide prompt casualty evacuation. Both the company and battalion commander had the means to coordinate fire support, including close air support, through their attached fire support officers. However, by committing to this course of action, the commanders could possibly find themselves in the thick of combat similar to the garrison at COP Tampa and unable to coordinate battalion- and company-level actions.

*   *   *

Both Kurilla and Hossfeld decided to move immediately to COP Tampa while coordinating reinforcements and supporting fires, using the firepower and armored protection of the Strykers to get through enemy fire at the outpost. The battalion TAC/Recon group immediately reversed direction and proceeded westward on Route LEXUS and turned northward onto MSR TAMPA, retracing the steps it had taken minutes before. The C TAC group, being in a more compact neighborhood, was unable to turn around quite as easily. Nevertheless, the four-vehicle group did soon reverse itself and began retracing its earlier route. Hossfeld soon saw the battalion TAC/Recon group in front of him. As his vehicle was turning back onto MSR TAMPA, a new explosion reverberated in the direction of the battalion TAC/ Recon group. The AIF were not through yet.[41]

Within minutes of turning north onto MSR TAMPA, the battalion TAC/Recon group found itself in the middle of the kill zone of a multiple IED ambush. The area was a stretch of road that both the battalion TAC/ Recon and C TAC groups had traveled in the opposite direction just minutes before. In the intervening time, the insurgents had established an ambush, planting seven IEDs, positioning a remotely detonated car bomb,

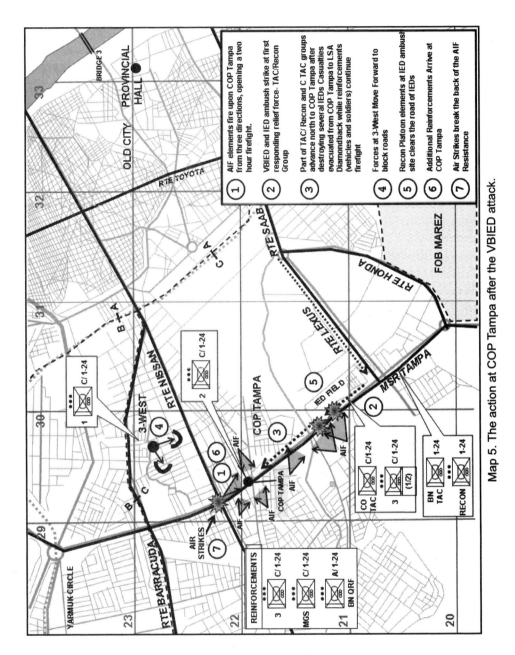

Map 5. The action at COP Tampa after the VBIED attack.

and moving up a suicide car bomber, all awaiting the expected return of the American force in response to the attack on COP Tampa. The lead element of the TAC/Recon group rode into the ambush. As observers in the lead Stryker spotted the IEDs composed of 120-mm and 155-mm artillery rounds rigged with tripwire detonators in the road, they radioed a warning to the rest of the group. At this point, the car bomber emerged and detonated his vehicular weapon against the second Stryker, HQ 203, the vehicle of the Recon Platoon's 3d Squad in which rode the platoon leader, 1LT John Bourque, setting off the ambush.[42]

The explosion extensively damaged the Stryker, disabling it. However, none of the Soldiers inside were seriously injured, although four were wounded. From the cover of buildings several hundred meters to the west of the highway, AIF elements opened with sporadic small-arms fire on the battalion TAC/Recon group. Despite this setback, Kurilla still felt the urgency to get to COP Tampa, so he decided to split his force. He left most of the Recon Platoon with two Strykers (in addition to the disabled one) behind, under Bourque, to deal with the casualties from the VBIED and to deal with the IED field. Meanwhile, the battalion TAC (Kurilla's own vehicle, HQs 66, and Bieger's S3 vehicle, HQs 63) along with the Recon Platoon's 1st Squad (in HQs 201, with the Recon Platoon's sergeant, SFC Robert Bowman, in charge), the lead vehicle at the time of the ambush, continued to the outpost.[43]

Hossfeld's C TAC group now arrived at the scene and the Cobra commander similarly divided his force. To provide security and medical support for the Recon Platoon element at the ambush site, he detached one of the two 3d Platoon vehicles, with the platoon sergeant, SFC James Maine, and the platoon medic, along with the vehicle of the company's fire support team. C TAC's remaining two vehicles (C66 and C34) then followed the BN TAC group at a short interval. This combined group moved west off MSR TAMPA along a dirt trail and, from a distance, fired .50-caliber machine guns and MK19s at two IEDs on the highway to set them off and create a clear passage to the north. One IED exploded and the second caught fire. The five vehicles then returned to MSR TAMPA and continued north to COP Tampa, receiving no further small arms fire until reaching the vicinity of the COP.[44]

Once at the outpost, the vehicles deployed to add their firepower to the defense. Bowman positioned HQs 201 in the northbound lane of MSR TAMPA just beyond the outpost, facing north. Kurilla placed his command vehicle, HQs 66, to the left of Bowman's vehicle on the highway median strip, facing to the west and northwest. Bieger pulled HQs 63 behind the battalion commander's vehicle, immediately in front of the COP to facilitate casualty evacuation. The two C Company vehicles, following the headquarters vehicles, halted just short of the COP and covered the south side, with the 3d Platoon vehicle (C34) moving close to the buildings just south of the COP itself. Kurilla now took personal command of the vehicles dueling with the enemy outside the building. Rockwell retained command of the Soldiers inside the building. Meanwhile, Hossfeld and Bieger moved into the building to determine the status of the garrison. Hossfeld immediately reinforced the COP with the squad from 3d Platoon. Moving from the vehicles to the building exposed the reinforcements to small arms fire, although no one was hit at this time.

Bieger, Hossfeld, and Soldiers from the 2d Platoon loaded the critically wounded personnel from the 2d Platoon, including Sanchez, into HQs 63, while under enemy small arms fire. Bieger departed and immediately drove the 4 miles south through the gauntlet of IEDs and the ambush site to the Army hospital located at LSA Diamondback, saving the lives of two of the Soldiers. Unfortunately, Sanchez died en route. Hossfeld followed Bieger, intent on organizing and bringing forward Cobra Company reinforcements and checking on the casualties. Almost immediately, an RPG fired from the west hit the Cobra command Stryker, taking out one of its front tires. This slowed Hossfeld's return. While moving, he coordinated over radio with the company executive officer who organized the reinforcements. These included the rest of the 3d Platoon, led by 1LT James Weaver (two Strykers with two squads and four machine guns), the company MGS platoon, led by 1LT Orlando Roy (three TOW Strykers), and the company XO's Stryker. After a quick trip to the combat support hospital, both Bieger and Hossfeld returned to battle. Hossfeld met his company XO, CPT Phon Sundra, and the eight Stykers (including the two left behind at the ambush site) assembled along MSR TAMPA outside the gate of FOB Marez, south of the ambush site. Hossfeld swapped Strykers with the company XO who remained behind at the company tactical operations center (TOC) on Marez.[45]

While the battle at COP Tampa continued, AIF fire at the ambush site began increasing in intensity, particularly after the insurgents realized the Americans were not going to be tricked into driving over IED tripwires. Under this now-heavy fire, two noncommissioned officers from the 2d Squad of the Recon Platoon, SSG Wesley Holt and SGT Joseph Martin, systematically detonated the five remaining IEDs. This cleared the route for both the Cobra Company reinforcements and a platoon from Apache Company, serving as the battalion's QRF, to move to COP Tampa. Bieger, too, returned to the fight at this time.[46]

With these reinforcements and close air support sorties provided by Navy F-14 Tomcats and Marine F/A-18s, the pressure on the 1-24 forces was alleviated.[47] The primary focus of the air strikes was against the AIF congregated near the intersection of MSR TAMPA and Route NISSAN.

Several airstrikes and TOW missile shots were directed at buildings near this crossroads. Soon, insurgent fire petered out. Almost 4 hours after the action started, calm returned to western Mosul. At least 25 insurgents were killed while 1-24 casualties stood at 1 killed and 20 wounded. Of the 20 wounded, 17 were back in action within 2 weeks. Two Strykers were out of action, while another six had light damage.[48]

While Hossfeld was occupied with the security of COP Tampa, another of the company's outposts, the 1st Platoon's position at the 3-West police station, was only about 800 meters northeast of where the VBIED went off. This platoon, led by 1LT Sean Keneally, monitored the action on the battalion and company radio frequencies. The digital communications devices in the Strykers allowed him (and the rest of the leaders in the 1-24) to follow the movements of all the vehicles involved in the action. Accordingly, on his own initiative, Keneally left one of his three squads and their Stryker at the police station and pushed forward his remaining squads and his own Stryker toward COP Tampa. This blocked the roads south and southwest of 3-West, hindering retreat or attack routes for the AIF in action near the COP.[49]

Immediately following the action, Kurilla ordered the evacuation of COP Tampa. Cobra Company removed all its equipment, including generators and the stray dog that had become the company mascot, and returned to FOB Marez. The battalion commander faced the decision of whether to retain the outpost or permanently abandon it. Given its location in the midst of the enemy's most active area and the willingness of the AIF to fight large battles to eliminate the outpost, the fight on 29 December could be the prelude to similar fights, much as Yarmuk Circle, which had no permanent garrison. However, abandoning the post would send the message that the insurgents had won a victory, no matter how pyrrhic, and, perhaps, create an even greater crisis in the days before the election. Kurilla could also follow a third course—retain the COP, reinforce it with additional troops expected to arrive in Mosul for pre-election security, and enlargen the perimeter to discourage further VBIED attacks.

*   *   *

The Deuce Four commander ultimately chose to retain COP Tampa and expand its perimeter. When reinforcements became available, additional troops would be dispatched to the outpost. By 2000 on 29 December, two platoons from Apache Company were rebuilding the defenses while an Army National Guard engineer determined that the concrete structure was still sound. Cobra's 3d Platoon reoccupied the COP at 0700 on 30 December. A tank platoon, part of a unit moved up from LSA Anaconda in central Iraq, came to be permanently assigned to COP Tampa for the duration of its existence as an American post.[50] The perimeter of the COP was expanded across MSR TAMPA, completely blocking the road until after the elections. Following the election, traffic was restricted to one lane southbound only. COP Tampa was transferred to ISF control not long after that.[51]

Soldiers in the 1st Battalion, 24th Infantry, earned 181 Purple Heart Medals during their yearlong tour of duty in Mosul. Of these, 20 or almost 10 percent were awarded for the action at COP Tampa. Three of the 5 Silver Stars and 11 of the 31 Bronze Stars for Valor awarded to unit members came from the same action. Many observers, including Kurilla himself, considered this action to be the turning point in the 1-24's fight in Mosul.[52] A month later, the Sunni Mansour district in southwest Mosul, not far from COP Tampa and the ambush site, had the highest voter turnout in all of northern Iraq.[53]

The AIF mastermind of the COP Tampa action, Mohammed Khalif Sharkawa, was fittingly captured by members of Cobra Company and Special Operations Forces (SOF) on 14 June 2005 in western Mosul. Sharkawa was found using information received from his own family and a previously captured colleague. His replacement in western Mosul, Abu Zayd, sent a letter to Iraqi al-Qaeda head Zarqawi a month later, lamenting the decline in insurgent attacks in Mosul. The letter also bemoaned the replacement of well planned and executed suicide attacks with more numerous, but less effective, suicide attacks employing poorly trained operatives. The document showed the distinct lack of leadership and organization existing in the AIF in the Mosul vicinity. The insurgents had shot their bolt at COP Tampa months earlier.[54]

Notes

1. The platoon leader was 1LT Sean Keneally, who led the 1st Platoon, C Company, 1-24th Infantry during the COP Tampa fight. See Kevin Graman, "Soldiers Says Most Iraqis in Mosul 'Grateful We are There,'" *The* (Spokane) *Spokesman Review*, 18 March 2005, online at <http://www.spokesmanreview.com/local/story.asp?ID=59669>, accessed 19 September 2006.

2. This is a 2003 population estimate. See "Iraq" in the *Information Please Almanac*, online at <http://www.infoplease.com/ipa/A0107644.html>, accessed 12 June 2006.

3. Mike Tucker, *Among Warriors in Iraq: True Grit, Special Ops, and Raiding in Mosul and Fallujah* (Guilford, CT: Lyons Press, 2005), 3–4.

4. United States Army Infantry School, *Infantry in Battle: From Somalia to the Global War on Terror* (Fort Benning, GA: United States Army Infantry School, 2005), 174–175.

5. FOB Marez or portions of it were previously known as FOB Glory, Camp Performance, and Camp Alabama. It was named in February 2004 after a retired command sergeant major of the 1st Battalion, 23d Infantry, who had recently died. See "18th Engineer Company," *The Arrowhead: Family Readiness Group Newsletter*, vol. 7, 22 February 2004, 12, online at <http://www.strykernews.com/docs/021904newsletter.pdf>, accessed 19 June 2006.

6. Kirsten Lundberg, "The Accidental Statesman: General Patraeus and the City of Mosul, Iraq," Kennedy School of Government Case Program C15-06-1834.0, John F. Kennedy School of Government, Harvard University, Cambridge, MA, 2006, 4. The 2d Brigade was actually in Mosul, along with the division headquarters, support units, and aviation. The 1st Brigade was at Qayyarrah-West, an airfield about 50 miles south of Mosul and the 3d Brigade was at the Tal Afar airfield about 30 miles west of Mosul.

7. The size disparity was really not that noticeable in Mosul itself. The 101st used a brigade in Mosul with a battalion on each side of the Tigris, as did the follow-on units. The disparity was much more apparent in other parts of Nineveh province where battalions replaced the other two 101st Brigades.

8. Erik Kurilla, personal e-mail message, 30 May 2006. LTC Michael Gibler, interview by the Operational Leadership Experiences (OLE) Project Team, Combat Studies Institute, digital recording, 8 June 2006, Fort Leavenworth, KS. [Digital recording stored on CD-ROM at Combined Arms Research Library, Fort Leavenworth, KS.]

9. Originally only C Company, 1-24, was assigned to western Mosul, attached to the 2d Squadron, 14th Cavalry (2-14 Cav). The bulk of 1-24 was assigned to the city of Tal Afar, about 30 miles west of Mosul. However, within weeks of the early October deployment of the 1st Brigade, 25th Infantry Division, the decision was made to swap the cavalry squadron with the 1-24. The swap was completed by 31 October 2004. See Christopher Hossfeld, telephone interview by author, 10 September 2006.

10. The 1-24 was reflagged from the former 3-9th Infantry at Fort Lewis in

August 1995 as part of an Army-wide reflagging campaign that saw the Army reduced in size from 12 to 10 divisions. This change was in conjunction with the replacement of the 1st Brigade, 7th Infantry Division, with the 1st Brigade, 25th Infantry Division, at Fort Lewis. The 1st Brigade, 7th Infantry Division, had been at Fort Lewis since 1994. During the reduction of the Army from 14 to 12 divisions in 1993, the whole 7th Infantry Division was designated to move from Fort Ord, CA, to Fort Lewis, but this was later whittled down to a brigade with the rest of the 7th Division inactivating. See the following: Jim Tice, "7th ID Soldiers Start Packing Their Bags," *Army Times*, 3 May 1993, 8; Jon Anderson, "Laying Down the 'Bayonet': Shutdown of Fort Ord, Inactivation of 7th ID a Massive Heartbreaker," *Army Times*, 13 September 1993, 28; Bernard Adelsberger, "Fort Lewis: Home for Two Heavy Brigades?" *Army Times*, 22 November 1993, 10; Sean Naylor, "The 10-Division Army: All the Details on What Stays and What Goes," *Army Times*, 12 December 1994, 12–13, 16; Sean Naylor, "What's in a Name? Inactivations Stir Memories of Old Soldiers," *Army Times*, 27 February 1995, 8, 10–11; Jim Tice, "All is Said and Done: New Flags for 172 Units," *Army Times*, 3 July 1995, 32, 38, 40, 42–44, 60.

11. Sean Naylor, "Radical Changes: Gen. Shinseki Unveils his 21st-Century Plans," *Army Times*, 25 October 1999, 8.

12. In a Stryker infantry platoon, two vehicles were equipped with the .50-caliber machine gun and two vehicles, the vehicles of the platoon leader and platoon sergeant, were equipped with the MK19. The platoon's two machine gun teams usually rode in these vehicles, giving them an M240 machine gun to use in the Stryker's air guard hatch. See Hossfeld interview.

13. Lester Grau and Elena Stoyanov, "The Bear Facts: Russians Appraise the Stryker Brigade Concept," *Infantry* 93 (November–December 2004), 38–40.

14. Michael Erik Kurilla, "Strykers Get the Job Done," Letter to the Editor, *Washington Post*, 5 April 2005, A22, online at <http://www.washingtonpost.com/wp-dyn/articles/A26535-2005Apr4.html>, accessed 7 June 2006.

15. Kurilla e-mail.

16. Vanantwerp replaced CPT William Jacobsen who was killed in the 21 December 2004 suicide bombing of the dining hall at FOB Marez.

17. Sources for Stryker unit organization include Department of the Army, Field Manual 3-21.21, *The Stryker Brigade Combat Team Infantry Battalion* (Washington, DC: Department of the Army, 2003); Department of the Army, Field Manual 3-21.11, *The SBCT Infantry Rifle Company* (Washington, DC: Department of the Army, 2003).

18. Ibid; Michael Yon, "The Battle for Mosul," *Michael Yon Online Magazine*, 14 May 2005, online at <http://www.michaelyon-online.com/wp/the-battle-for-mosul.htm>, accessed 1 June 2006; Michael Knights, "Northern Iraq Faces Increased Instability in 2005," *Jane's Intelligence Review*, February 2005, 30–33, online at <http://www.washingtoninstitute.org/opedsPDFs/4216175bf103e.pdf>, accessed 7 July 2006; Yon, "The Battle for Mosul."

19. Ibid.

20. "Deuce Four Fallen Warriors," *Stryker Brigade News*, 21 February

2005, online at <http://www.strykernews.com/archives/2005/02/21/deuce_four_fallen_warriors.html>, accessed 31 August 2006. The KIA was SPC Thomas Doerflinger.

21. Gibler interview.

22. Kurilla e-mail; Knights, 32–33. Hossfeld interview; Christopher Hossfeld, personal e-mail message, 19 September 2006. A brief timeline of large actions involving the 1-24 in November–December 2004:

10–13 November	First Battle of Yarmuk Circle.
14–29 November	Ongoing campaign to regain control of Mosul nets 43 insurgent detainees.
1 December	Large gun battle.
3 December	Three hour firefight on Route Tampa against 2-kilometer-long ambush.
11 December	Rocket and mortar attack at a check-point followed by an unsuccessful ambush results in the first Silver Star being awarded to a 1-24 member: SSG Shannon Key.
13 December	Second Battle of Yarmuk Circle.
21 December	Homicide bomber attacks dining facility at FOB Mosul, killing 22 including two 1-24 Infantry Soldiers, one being the A Company Commander, CPT William Jacobsen.
22–24 December	Multicompany Operation Vicksburg in Bulldog Company sector north of Yarmuk Circle with supporting operations south of the circle.
28 December	Insurgents tried to seize a western Mosul police station and are repelled, primarily by ISF elements; this was the ninth such unsuccessful attempt since 10 November.
29 December	Action at COP Tampa.

23. Hossfeld interview.

24. Michael Yon. "The Battle for Mosul: Dispatch II." *Michael Yon Online Magazine*, 21 May 2005, online at <http://www.michaelyon-online.com/wp/the-battle-for-mosul-dispatch-ii.htm>, accessed 1 June 2006. These extremist groups were Abu Musab al-Zarqawi's al-Qaeda affiliated "Al Qaeda in Mesopotamia," formerly called *Jama'at Al-Tawhid wa Al-Jihad, Ansar al-Islam, Al-Jihad,* and the *Mujahidin Shura* Council and the *Ansar Al-Sunnah* Army. The latter organization took credit for the 21 December bombing of the FOB Marez dining facility. See Knights, 32.

25. Yon, "The Battle for Mosul: Dispatch II."

26. Hossfeld interview; Knights, 32; Michael Gilbert, "Silver Star Goes

56

to Stryker Soldiers Tested in Iraq," *The* (Tacoma) *News Tribune*, 6 November 2005, online at <http://www.thenewstribune.com/news/local/story/5312151p-4814745c.html>, accessed 9 June 2006.

27. Richard A. Oppel, Jr., "U.S. and Iraqi Troops Capture a Top Militant Leader in Mosul," *New York Times*, 17 June 2005, A13, online at <http://proquest. umi.com/pqdweb?did=855023721&sid=1&Fmt=3&clientId=5094&RQT=309& VName=PQD>, accessed 14 September 2006; Knights, 32; Gibler interview.

28. Jeffrey Vanantwerp, personal e-mail message, 3 June 2006; Jeffrey Vanantwerp, "AO Apache," PowerPoint slide, 3 June 2006; Scott Cheney, personal e-mail message, 25 June 2006; Scott Cheney, "C 1-24 Boundaries," PowerPoint slide, 25 June 2006; Matthew McGrew, personal e-mail message, 24 July 2006); Christopher Hossfeld, "C Company Commander, COP Tampa," PowerPoint presentation, 12 September 2006.

29. Kurilla e-mail; Vanantwerp e-mail.

30. Gilbert; Vanantwerp e-mail; Hossfeld interview; Scott Killpack, "Memoirs of a Soldier 3," Internet Blog,1 April 2006, online at <http://myspace. com/killpack>, accessed 7 September 2006; Hossfeld e-mail.

31. The Army found the legitimate owner of the building and contracted with him for a monthly rental fee for its use. See Hossfeld e-mail.

32. Dionne Searcy, "Holding the Fort, Losing a Friend in Suicide Bombing," *Newsday*, 3 January 2005, online at <http://www.newsday.com/news/nationworld/ world/ny-wobatt0103,0,3976293,print.story>, accessed 15 September 2006; Killpack, "Memoirs of a Soldier 2," Internet Blog, 1 April 2006, online at <http:// myspace.com/killpack>, accessed 7 September 2006"; Hossfeld interview.

33. "Explosion Rocks Northwest Baghdad," American Forces Press Service, 29 December 2004, online at <http://www.defenselink.mil/news/Dec2004/ n12292004_2004122901.html>, accessed 15 September 2006. C Company Commander CPT Chris Hossfeld was wounded by an RPG shot at his Stryker on 24 December in Yarmuk Circle. See Hossfeld interview.

34. Hossfeld interview; Killpack, "Memoirs of a Soldier 3."

35. Hossfeld interview; Hossfeld, "C Company Commander, COP Tampa."

36. Ibid.; Killpack, "Memoirs of a Soldier 3."

37. Hossfeld interview; Graman.

38. Hossfeld interview. The al-Qaeda in Mesopotamia attack video, COP Tampa VBIED Full.mpg, can be viewed at "COP Tampa VBIED Full.mpg," online at <http://www.megaupload.com/?d=L8SSAYGO>, accessed 11 September 2006.

39. Hossfeld interview.

40. Ibid.; Gilbert; Michelle Tan, "Heavy Mettle Tour: Deuce Four's Extraordinary Commitment to One Another and Their Mission Earned Them Numerous Awards—and Iraqi's Trust," *Army Times*, 27 March 2006, 15–16.

41. Hossfeld interview; Hossfeld, "C Company Commander, COP Tampa."

42. Tan, 15–16; 1st Battalion, 24th Infantry, "1-24 IN COP Tampa Complex Attack," PowerPoint slide, 2005.

43. Ibid.

44. Hossfeld interview; Hossfeld, "C Company Commander, COP Tampa."

45. Tan, 15–16; 1st Battalion, 24th Infantry, "1-24 IN COP Tampa Complex Attack," PowerPoint slide, 2005; Hossfeld interview.

46. Ibid. Holt and Martin, along with Bieger, were later awarded the Silver Star for their actions on 29 December. Eleven Bronze Stars for Valor awarded to 1-24 Soldiers during the unit's 1-year tour in Mosul, 11 were awarded for actions on 29 December. The 11 Soldiers so honored were 2d Platoon Leader 1LT Jeremy Rockwell, 2d Platoon SFC Mark Gallegos, 2d Platoon Squad Leaders SSG Robert Bernsten and SSG Joseph Robeson (who was also badly wounded), and 2d Platoon members SGT Nicholas Furfari, SGT Brandon Huff, SGT Christopher Manikowski, SPC Dennis Burke, SPC Steven Sosa, and, posthumously, PFC Oscar Sanchez. Recon Platoon Leader 1LT John Bourne also received a Bronze Star for Valor.

47. 1st Battalion, 24th Infantry, "1-24 IN COP Tampa Complex Attack"; Tan; Gilbert. Kurilla had been calling in air strikes as early as the evacuation of the first casualties.

48. Hossfeld interview; 1st Battalion, 24th Infantry, "1-24 IN COP Tampa Complex Attack"; Gilbert.

49. Hossfeld interview.

50. The tank unit was the M1 equipped Company B, 1st Battalion, 185th Armor, a California Army National Guard unit normally assigned to the 81st Infantry Brigade (Mechanized). See "12 February 2005," online at <http://iraq-kill-maim.org/ik35/iraq-kill35.htm>, accessed 1 August 2006; Hossfeld interview.

51. Hossfeld interview.

52. Kurilla e-mail; Gilbert.

53. Sandra Jonz, "Soldiers Look to Gain, Secure Trust with Iraqis," *Stars and Stripes*, Mideast edition, 28 May 2005, online at <http://www.google.com/search?q=cache:ko3th_Ik5MMJ:www.stripes.com/article.asp%3Fsection%3D104%26article%3D29384+Mosul&hl=en&gl=us&ct=clnk&cd=58>, accessed 16 May 2006.

54. "Terrorist Letter Claims Poor Leadership in Mosul," Multinational Force-Iraq Release A050806, 6 August 2005, online at <http://www.globalsecurity.org/military/library/news/2005/08/mil-050806-mnfi02.htm>, accessed 1 August 2006.

Palm Sunday Ambush, 20 March 2005

by

Thomas A. Bruscino, Jr.

Just before noon on 20 March 2005—Palm Sunday—a large group of insurgents launched a complex ambush on two Coalition convoys as they converged on a highway 26 miles southeast of Baghdad. The attack came nearly 2 years into the American-led Coalition campaign in Iraq, a few months after the Coalition drove the insurgents from their stronghold in Fallujah in November 2004, and 2 months after the Iraqi people held a free election in January 2005. Throughout the operations in Iraq, Coalition forces faced the constant struggle of maintaining open and secure supply lines. The insurgents sought to disrupt those supply lines. More importantly, the insurgents knew supply routes provided opportunities to launch attacks that would inflict casualties—casualties they hoped would break down the Coalition's will to fight.

The US Army had become well aware of the threat to convoy operations over the first 2 years of the war. By the spring of 2005, Army vehicles accompanied most convoys. Sometimes Army tractor-trailers were interspersed among the civilian trucks. Oftentimes, Army guntrucks—uparmored high-mobility multipurpose wheeled vehicles (HMMWVs) or larger armored trucks—escorted the convoys, keeping an eye out for ambushes and roadside bombs, known to the military as improvised explosive devises (IEDs). The enemy, recognizing the growing American proficiency in resisting ambushes, had shifted tactics, which led to the proliferation of IEDs across the country. When the insurgents did launch ambushes, small groups of 7 to 10 men made the attack, inflicted as many casualties as possible, and then made a hasty retreat, often in prearranged vehicles.[1]

Apparently unsatisfied with the results of these smaller operations, in March 2005 one group of insurgents decided to increase the stakes and go for more spectacular victories. On 18 March, that group, numbering approximately 50 men, assaulted a 30-vehicle convoy southeast of Baghdad, damaging as many as half of the vehicles and killing at least one civilian driver. They got away before Coalition reinforcements could arrive. Most likely, the same group launched the Palm Sunday ambush 2 days later.[2] They were a well-organized and well-armed force, and on 20 March they brought a variety of small arms, heavy machine guns, rocket propelled grenades (RPG), mortars, and at least one IED to the fight.

For the Palm Sunday ambush, the insurgents chose a section of highway east of Salman Pak, a town in a bend in the Tigris River named for one of Mohammad's companions and home to a notorious military training camp under the regime of Saddam Hussein.[3] The road, sometimes called Iraq Route 6, and known to the Americans as Alternate Supply Route DETROIT, was a four-lane paved highway separated by a dirt median. The highway ran generally north-south, and had become a key route on which to move men and supplies from the Baghdad area to all points south. At the site of the ambush, an access road ran westward, perpendicular to the main highway.[4] The surrounding area was mostly open, rural, scrub brush, desert terrain. South of the access road, there was more vegetation in the form of medium-sized trees. Among the trees, especially on the west side of the main route, were several structures within 150 meters of the road, including vendor stands, a brick building, and a two-story house—all of which provided excellent cover for about 15 of the insurgents. (See figure 2.)

North of the access road was more desolate open ground, even though a tree line paralleled the north side of the access road. Along the edge of the tree line, the ground rose to a berm and then dipped into a trench line. The tree and trench lines extended from roughly 230 meters down the access road to within 30 to 50 meters of the main road where the tree line tapered off. At that point, the trench made a 90 degree turn to the north and paralleled the main road for a few hundred meters. Within these L-shaped trench lines (to the northwest of the intersection of the main road and the access road) stood a small, undergrown orchard, spotted with roughly 40 trees and bushes in rows, about 160 meters off the main road. Farther to the southwest, about 350 meters off the main road and 350 meters from the access road, stood a large powerplant. The trenches, berms, and structures along the west side of the main road provided excellent cover for ambushing forces, and the insurgents placed the bulk of their force, about 35 men, in that area.

Coalition forces included two convoys and their escorts (see figure 3). The northbound convoy was a mixed Army and civilian force numbering 32 vehicles: 22 civilian tractor-trailers interspersed with 7 Army trucks from the 1075th Transportation Company, each manned by two Soldiers. Three HMMWV convoy escort platforms from the 518th Guntruck Company (Provisional), under the call sign Regulator, each manned by three Soldiers, and each with a mounted M2 .50-caliber machine gun, escorted the convoy.[5] Regulator 1 was at the front of the convoy, Regulator 2 was in the middle, and Regulator 3 was in the rear. Immediately behind Regulator 1 was the vehicle carrying the convoy commander from the

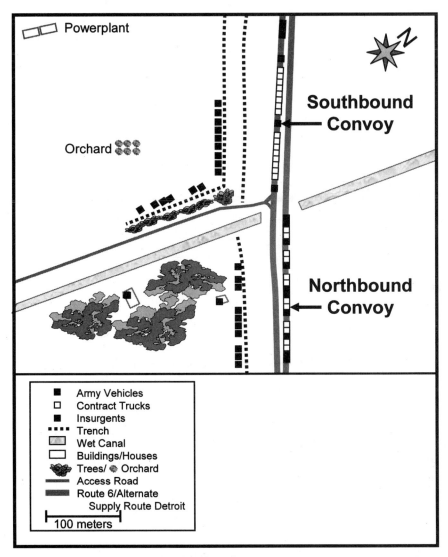

Figure 2. Ambush site.

1075th, SSG Jeffrey Uhl. Less than 2 miles south of the ambush site, the convoy passed through an Iraqi-run checkpoint. There some Soldiers noticed strange activity, including an Iraqi guardsman holding a large RPG launcher, but not enough to raise suspicions about the road ahead.[6]

The all-civilian southbound convoy consisted of 30 tractor-trailers, an Army and Air Force Exchange Service (AAFES) bus, and 2 Ford Sport Utility Vehicles (SUVs), escorted by 3 HMMWVs from Battery B, 1st Battalion, 623d Field Artillery (FA) Regiment, call sign Stallion 33. The

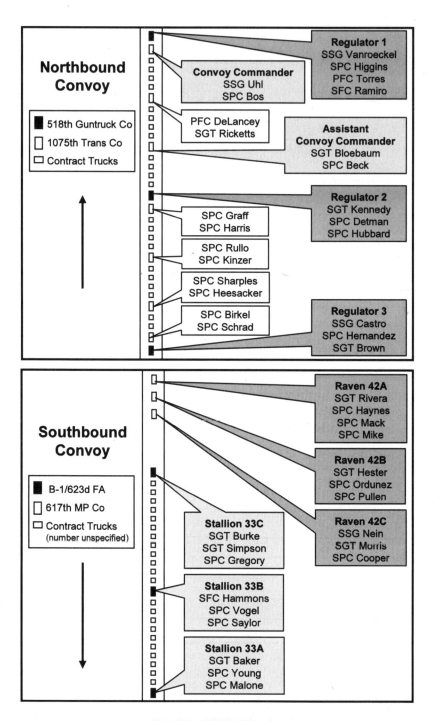

Figure 3. Convoy layout.

southbound convoy was traveling along a sector of the road guarded by the 617th Military Police (MP) Company. On 20 March, 2d Squad, 4th Platoon, 617th MP Company was in the area, and began shadowing the southbound convoy. The MP squad consisted of three HMMWVs. Three Soldiers manned the first vehicle, including the squad leader, SSG Timothy F. Nein, and they had a .50-caliber machine gun as the crew-served weapon. The second vehicle also carried three Soldiers, led by vehicle commander SGT Leigh Ann Hester, and had a MK19 grenade launcher and a M240B machine gun as their dual-mounted crew-served weapons. The third HMMWV also carried a .50-caliber machine gun and four Soldiers, including the unit medic.[7]

Working under the call sign Raven 42, the three HMMWVs from the 617th MP Company had been patrolling their 15- to 25-mile long section of the highway for most of the morning when they came upon the southbound convoy. The MPs made radio contact with the southbound convoy and informed them they were going to shadow them through the rest of their area. The MPs had plenty of experience with that highway. They had arrived in Iraq in November 2004 and took over for another MP unit providing security for the main roads southeast of Baghdad. Most mornings they would patrol the area to look for ambush sites or roadside bombs. Then, as the convoys began moving through the region, the MPs would either escort or shadow the trucks until they moved on to another unit's sector.

The Soldiers of the 2d Squad, 4th Platoon took their responsibilities very seriously, and prepared vigorously for the job under the leadership of their company commander, CPT Todd Lindner, and their squad leader Nein. Because they usually operated as a squad in three vehicles, Nein and his three team leaders, SGT Joe Rivera, Hester, and SGT Dustin Morris, proved particularly important in their preparation for action. In the weeks and months after their arrival in Iraq, the squad performed preventative maintenance checks and services after every mission, no matter how long or vigorous the mission. They cleared the vehicles of any unnecessary equipment that might slow down the unit under fire. They made their vehicles as uniform as possible, storing the arms, ammunition, and equipment in all three HMMWVs in the exact same places and in the exact same way to ensure that under fire any member of the squad could find what he or she needed without hesitation.

Nein insisted that they go over the routes and route maps repeatedly, making sure that every member of his squad knew the terrain backward and forward. Then they rehearsed, both on the road and in front of dry erase boards. Nein and his team leaders pointed out intersections that were likely ambush sites, discussing what to do in the event of an attack at any of those sites. The squad ran through every scenario they could think of: when to attack and when to get out of the kill zone, when to dismount and when to stay in the vehicle, who would provide covering fire, and what to do if they lost a vehicle.

The squad also had experience with actions along the route. On 27 January, a small group of insurgents attacked them at night. After a brief exchange of fire, during which no one on either side was killed or wounded, the enemy broke contact and disappeared. Two days later, while patrolling the highway early in the morning, they ran into a group of 7 to 10 insurgents setting up an ambush. The enemy opened fire, and after a 15-minute firefight, the MPs captured two insurgents, one of them wounded. The rest got away by running through the canal system and the heavy foliage in the area. Even though the Americans took no casualties in the action, they were disappointed with their efforts that day. Morris recalled they had horrible communications that threw off all their actions: "We didn't attack as soon as we should have and I don't think we were forceful enough. That was a big issue in a lot of the insurgents getting away and us only capturing two of them." The lessons were clear, "be better organized, attack as soon as you can, dismount when you need to dismount, stay in the trucks when you need to stay in the trucks, and not have everybody do their own thing as much."[8] The squad, already frustrated by what they saw as their sub-par performance, just missed getting into the defense against the 18 March insurgent attack on the convoy in their sector southeast of Baghdad.[9] But all of their preparation, experience, and frustration would come together 2 days later, on Sunday, 20 March 2005.

Palm Sunday was a clear, calm, mostly sunny day with temperatures in the mid-70s to mid-80s. Shortly before noon, the two convoys came together on Iraq Route 6. Both had been driving all morning; both still had several hours ahead of them. By some chance, the two convoys were to cross paths right at the access road in the middle of the ambush kill zone. They were almost nose-to-nose when the firing started.

Just as they passed the access road, the team chief of the lead HMMWV in the southbound convoy saw two black-clad men rise on the right side of the main route. One of the men lifted an RPG launcher to his shoulder, took aim, and fired. The ground and fields to the right of the convoy came alive with small arms fire. As bullets pinged off the side of the vehicle, the lead HMMWV, call sign Stallion 33A, sped up to guide the trucks out of the kill zone, the gunner firing his MK19 grenade launcher at the attackers. Two loud explosions shook the ground behind them. The AAFES bus, apparently struck by an IED, rose, flipped in the air, and rolled into the median. Farther back, one of the Ford SUVs tried to accelerate, but machine gun fire dotted the passenger side door and shattered the windshield. The rounds caused the driver to swerve across the median and wreck the truck.

The lead HMMWV drove on south, continuing to give and take fire for at least a half mile. It continued on to the Iraqi checkpoint that the northbound convoy had just left, almost 2 miles down the road. When Stallion 33A came to a stop, the men in the HMMWV realized that only one vehicle had followed them. The Soldiers told the truck driver to stay at the checkpoint, and radioed their squad leader for instructions. He told them they were needed on the battlefield, so they headed back north. Their convoy was still in the kill zone.[10]

Almost as soon as the attack began, one of the lead tractor-trailers in the southbound convoy was disabled. The rest of the drivers stopped their trucks, most of them directly in line with the main ambush site north of the access road. With their vehicles taking a beating, many of the civilian drivers left their cabs and tried to find cover on the left side of their trucks, east of the highway. Stallion 33B, the middle HMMWV in the convoy carrying squad leader SFC Rickie Hammons, also felt the force of the attack. For the first part of the fight, they held their position and periodically returned fire on the insurgent positions. When the situation did not improve, they moved their HMMWV forward on the right side of the highway toward Stallion 33A's original position at the front of the convoy. The vehicle took heavy fire the entire way, but the Soldiers could not make out the specific insurgent positions, so the gunner tried to lay down suppressive fire to the right with his .50-caliber machine gun. By the time they reached the front of the convoy, the lead HMMWV had moved on to the Iraqi checkpoint, and they found that all the lead vehicles, including the bus and both SUVs, had been destroyed. They continued down the road about half a mile, firing to the right as they went.[11] Stallion 33C, the rear HMMWV escort in the southbound convoy, also took fire from the right. They too held their position and tried to return fire. Later, when the enemy fire died down at the rear of the convoy, Stallion 33C headed toward the front of the convoy, using the northbound lane. None of the Soldiers in the southbound convoy could figure out a way to get their convoy moving again.[12]

"S___! Contact left!" The driver of Regulator 1, the lead guntruck in the northbound convoy, heard the shots strike the driver's side of her vehicle and shouted the news into the radio. After stopping at the shock of the initial assault, she pulled the vehicle forward and to the left side of the northbound lane and stopped south of the access road. The three other Soldiers opened fire on targets in the trenches and among the structures on the left side of the road. Within minutes, the M2 .50-caliber machine gun jammed, and the gunner switched to the M249 Squad Automatic Weapon (SAW). The sergeant in the passenger seat dismounted and fired his M16 rifle over the hood of the vehicle.[13]

While Regulator 1 stopped to draw fire and engage the attackers, its convoy came to a screeching halt. The convoy commander, Uhl, riding in the tractor-trailer directly behind Regulator 1, later said the guntruck "stopped for only a few seconds. But it was long enough that we had to stop."[14] Then one of the SUVs from the southbound convoy swerved across the median, crashed into a civilian car that had pulled over to allow the northbound convoy to pass, and ended up sideways blocking the north-bound lane. In the chaos, Uhl did not realize the SUV was a wounded friendly. Fearing that the disabled Ford was part of the ambush, Uhl ordered his driver, SPC Tim Bos, to ram the SUV out of the way, spinning it back toward the median. With that obstacle gone, the lead tractor-trailer left the kill zone. "We were out of the kill zone," Uhl recalled. "And at that point, I figured that everyone would just follow. But that didn't happen." No one followed, and the frustrated convoy commander was forced to listen to the rest of the fight on the radio. He set up a casualty collection point a mile or so up the road and waited.[15]

The civilian tractor-trailers behind the northbound convoy commander were not moving. One had gotten itself stuck diagonally in the muddy median, directly in front of the disabled SUV; another simply stopped on the right side of the road. To get away from the fire, contract drivers from throughout the convoy jumped out of their trucks and hid behind the tires or in ditches along the road. Caught up in the crush of vehicles, the second Army tractor-trailer in the convoy became a target of opportunity for the insurgents south of the access road. The armored doors stopped most of the incoming shots, but before long a bullet passed through the hinge on the door and struck the driver, SGT Terry Ricketts, in the leg. He yelled, "I'm hit! I'm hit!" into the radio, while his co-driver, PFC Ricky DeLancey, tried to find a target with his SAW.[16]

As the battle intensified, Regulator 2, the second guntruck in the north-bound convoy, pulled out to the left of the formation and moved ahead four or five trucks, all the while shooting toward the insurgent positions on the left side of the road. The Soldiers intended to draw fire away from the convoy, but to do so, they themselves became a conspicuous target for the insurgents. Almost as soon as they stopped, a round hit the driver, SPC Ryan Hubbard, in the abdomen. The gunner tried to lay down suppressive fire with his .50-caliber machine gun, but like the M2 on Regulator 1, the machine gun kept jamming. More small arms fire raked the HMMWV. Suddenly, plumes of white smoke filled the vehicle. Later they would discover that the smoke came from a bullet hitting the fire extinguisher under the front seat, but at the time the clouds confused and frightened the crew. The vehicle commander, concerned about the mysterious smoke and the wounds to his driver, ordered Hubbard to reverse the vehicle toward the rear of the convoy. Hubbard complied, but passed in and out of consciousness due to his injuries. By the time they had moved back six or seven vehicles he had passed out, and the vehicle commander had to lift Hubbard's foot off the gas so the HMMWV would roll to a stop. The troops tried to provide suppressive fire from the rear of the convoy and they continued to be shot at from multiple points, but they were effectively out of the fight. The crew tended to their driver and looked for an opportunity to get him and their damaged vehicle out of the area.[17]

The insurgents now shifted their fire back to the front section of the northbound convoy, especially the stopped truck holding DeLancey and the wounded Ricketts. An explosive device slammed into their hood a few feet in front of the passenger seat. The explosion shattered the right front windshield, cutting DeLancey's face and burning his right shoulder. The blast also collapsed a portion of the truck's dashboard onto Ricketts, pinning him in his seat. As DeLancey tried to recover from the explosion and return fire, a bullet entered the left front of his helmet, skimmed the side of his head, and blew a hole out the back of the helmet. Shaken by the attacks, but strangely calm, he told Ricketts, "We're going to die." Ricketts replied, just as calm, "Yeah, I know." But rather than give up, DeLancey became enraged and said "F___ it."[18] He kicked out what was left of the windshield, crawled out on the hood, and opened fire with the SAW on any target he could find.[19]

Just to the rear of Ricketts and DeLancey, a contractor named Ron Hart was crouching down in the cab of his truck attempting to take cover from the small arms fire. As the bullets passed through his vehicle, Hart realized that he needed to find better cover, so he pulled his truck forward to take refuge beside the Army trailers carrying large containers. Hart stopped his vehicle on the right side of Ricketts and DeLancey's vehicle and jumped out to hide behind the Army truck. He saw the bloodied and exhausted DeLancey get out of the passenger side door and place his SAW on the ground. Hart, a retired Army noncommissioned officer, took the machine gun, told DeLancey to get down, and began firing at the insurgent positions from behind the wheels of the Army vehicle.[20]

The firing by DeLancey and Hart helped give some precious moments of relief to the battered convoy—enough time at least for Soldiers in the 1075th to try to get the trucks moving again. The third Army truck in the northbound convoy was driven by SPC Jennifer Beck and held the assistant convoy commander, SGT Anthony Bloebaum. At the casualty collection point, the convoy commander had grown anxious that none of the other vehicles had reached him yet. He radioed back his intent to return to the kill zone, but Bloebaum and Beck warned him off, insisting they would get the convoy moving again. Several of the tractor-trailers near the front of the convoy had finally started to move. Their movement freed up space for Beck and Bloebaum, who knew from the radio that Ricketts and DeLancey needed help. They pulled forward until they were to the right of Hart's civilian truck, and then radioed back to the vehicles behind them to get going.[21]

It did not take long for the next Army truck, driven by SPC Jacob Graff and SPC John Harris, to heed the call. They pulled to the right of the convoy and started to head out of the kill zone. The movement drew the attention of the insurgents. One account described what happened next:

> Harris was quickly hit in the neck, the bullet hitting an artery and leaving him unable to speak.
>
> "Are you OK?" Graff asked.
>
> Harris gestured to say yes.
>
> "You're not hurt?"
>
> Harris waived it off, no.
>
> "So you're not OK?"
>
> Harris finally just frantically pointed straight ahead, his gesture saying what his lips could not: Get us out of here![22]

A shot struck Graff in the shoulder, but he drove on. A few minutes later, several other trucks got out of the kill zone.[23]

The handful of vehicles that had left the northbound convoy passed Regulator 1 on their way to the casualty collection point. The Soldiers in the guntruck had their own problems. The .50-caliber kept jamming on the gunner, the vehicle commander had little experience with convoy escort duty, communications with the convoy were spotty at best, and no one took control of the situation. Nevertheless, they stayed in the kill zone throughout the early part of the fight, moving back and forth trying to find targets on the side of the road. Shortly after Graff and Harris left the kill zone, Regulator 1 followed, its gunner firing as it moved down the road. At the casualty collection point, the troops from Regulator 1 helped administer first aid to the wounded drivers; however, the bulk of the convoy had not made it out, and the trucks were rapidly running out of escorts to protect them.[24]

Both convoys now found themselves under intense fire. Near the front of the stalled southbound convoy, one of the lead tractor-trailers took a direct hit from an RPG and caught fire. Wisps of black smoke began to rise over the battlefield, directly in front of the main enemy position in the orchard. The disabled vehicles and terrified drivers made ready targets for the insurgents. In the middle of the kill zone, a running camera recorded the words of one of the civilian truck drivers: "Pretty much, we're scared s___less."[25] The insurgents began to press their advantage, moving forward across the field to a trench line closer to the main road.[26] Everything so far was going the insurgents' way.

The three vehicles of Raven 42, the Kentucky MPs, were 200 to 300 meters behind the southbound convoy on the morning of 20 March when they noticed that some of the trucks ahead had begun to wobble strangely.[27] The gunner in the lead HMMWV, SPC Casey Cooper, heard gunfire and explosions and yelled, "They're getting hit, Go! Go! Go! Go!"[28] Nein, the squad leader and lead vehicle commander, radioed the news back to the other two HMMWVs, and the driver, Morris, accelerated, switched to the northbound lanes, and sped down the left side of the convoy. As the squad neared the access road, about halfway through the convoy, they found a gap in the trucks and crossed back over to the right side of the southbound lane, between the convoy and the main body of insurgents. They immediately began taking fire from the insurgents, and the three gunners opened up with their crew-served weapons.

The access road was dead ahead. The MPs had several options at this point in the battle: they could have tried to keep moving and lead the convoy out of the kill zone; they could have stopped and tried to get the convoy moving again while providing suppressive fire from the main road; or they could have stopped short of the action and tried to call in close air support (CAS). But none of their extensive preparation or expectations led to those actions. Two days earlier the squad had done a reconnaissance of the access road and had discussed what they would do in the event of an ambush in that area. When they had run through their rehearsals, they had assumed that no more than 12 or 15 insurgents would participate in most ambushes—the standard operating procedure for the enemy over the previous months in Iraq. As the MPs approached the access road, they had no idea that they faced a force of at least 45 to 50 insurgents.[29] SPC Ashley Pullen, driver of the second vehicle, later said that if Nein "would have known that there were that many people there, he may have taken a different action."[30]

*   *   *

But by then it did not matter. As Raven 42 had rehearsed, and as the squad anticipated, Nein ordered Morris to turn down the access road, right into the teeth of the ambush. The MPs came onto the scene just as the group of insurgents moved forward across the field in front of the orchard, toward the southbound convoy. When the MPs made the turn, the enemy north of the access road focused all of their fire on the three HMMWVs. A hail of bullets and multiple RPG rounds slammed into the front and passenger side of the lead vehicle, and just as they made the right turn an RPG hit above the rear passenger door. The driver of the second HMMWV recalled that, "The truck was picked up off the ground and moved from the impact of the RPG."[31] The explosion knocked the gunner, Cooper, unconscious, and he fell face forward in his platform.[32]

Berms lined both sides of the access road. To the left of the MPs, the berm grew to a height of 6 to 10 feet with a wet canal on the other side. On the right the berm was only a few feet tall, but it was lined with medium-sized trees. On the other side of the berm was a trench that ran back toward the main road and connected in an L-shape with the main trench. Nein had Morris drive down the access road about 230 meters, to the end of the tree line. Where they stopped, a two-story house stood behind the tall berm on the left side of the road.

By the time the lead vehicle rolled to a stop, both front tires had gone flat, a round had penetrated the engine block, and oil was sputtering over the hood and windshield. Nein described the intensity of those initial moments:

> I turn around to check on Specialist Cooper and he's laying face down on his platform with his head in the foot well behind my seat. I shake him, he doesn't answer, and I believe he's dead. I begin to climb over the top of him, hoping the .50 caliber is still operable; and as I'm climbing over him, he springs back up, says he's okay,

and jumps back on the weapons system . . . at that point, I turn around and see seven cars. All four doors open on each and all [the] trunks. I do the math and realize we've got 28 guys out here at least. I start to call up [the CAS relay station] to tell him we need CAS immediately. . . .[33]

The second vehicle, driven by Pullen, pulled up 15 to 25 meters behind the first truck, and the gunners for both vehicles—the revived Cooper on his .50-caliber, and SPC Jesse Ordunez alternating among his MK19 grenade launcher, M240B machine gun, and SAW—continued shooting at insurgents in the field north of the access road. Their fire gave Nein, Morris, and Hester (the vehicle commander of the second HMMWV) the chance to dismount and take up firing positions with their M4 rifles along the berm on the right side of the road. Pullen dismounted and took up a firing position on the rear left side of her truck.[34]

The third MP truck did not follow all the way to the first two vehicles. The vehicle commander, Rivera, noticed that a large group of insurgents had taken up positions along the trench paralleling the main highway. He ordered his driver, SPC Brian Mack, to stop the HMMWV right at the end of the trench, about 25 to 35 meters down the access road. There the gunner, SPC Bill Haynes, opened fire on the trench with his .50-caliber, while Rivera, Mack, and the unit medic, SPC Jason Mike, dismounted and took up firing positions on the left side of the vehicle. The insurgents could see that they had no chance if they did not take out Rivera's truck, so they turned much of their attention to the third HMMWV. Mike saw firsthand the effects of the intense enemy fire:

> At that point SPC Mack had given me his M4 and he took SPC Haynes' M249 [SAW]. I begin to fire and that's when I heard SPC Mack yell out he was hit. I went over to him and uncovered his wound and observed a gunshot wound to the left arm. At that time I gave him a first aid bandage to put pressure on his wound and I put him into cover under the vehicle. SGT Rivera and SPC Haynes were still laying down suppressive fire to keep security. I then proceeded to fire because we were taking heavy fire from the trench still at this point. Soon after I begin shooting SGT Rivera yelled out he was hit and that he couldn't feel his legs.[35]

The round that struck Mack in the arm tumbled into his torso and lodged between his heart and lungs. A bullet had entered Rivera's abdomen, passing through his body and barely missing his spine. Within a few moments, Haynes also yelled that he was hit, having taken shrapnel in his left hand. Bleeding profusely, Haynes wrapped his hand with a bandage he got from the medic and continued firing the .50-caliber. While Mike tended to the wounded, bullets bounced off the pavement all around him, and he came to a realization—both Mack and Rivera had been behind cover when they were hit. The insurgents were on both sides of the road.[36]

At the same time, the lead vehicles also started taking fire from the south side of the access road. Cooper and Ordunez, the gunners in the lead and second vehicles, respectively, both heard the bullets coming from their rear. Ordunez had been firing at the field with his SAW when a round hit the machine gun, rendered it inoperable, and knocked him down into the truck. As he reloaded the M240B machine gun, he saw an enemy fighter brandishing an automatic weapon on the tall berm behind him. He thought, "This is the end; there's no way out," but managed to bring the gun around and fire on the insurgent, driving him down behind the berm.[37] Cooper called to Nein that they needed a grenade on the insurgent's position, so while Hester shot and killed an enemy fighter who jumped up on the north side of the road, Nein tossed a grenade over the berm on the south side. Worried that the insurgent might have survived, he scrambled up the berm and saw that the enemy was gone.

The MPs found themselves in a precarious situation. Despite the medic's frantic efforts to get their attention from his position down the road, the Soldiers in the first two vehicles did not yet realize that three of the four men in the third HMMWV were wounded, two of them seriously. Pullen first recognized something was wrong when she heard screaming over the radio inside her truck. Mike was calling for help, but in the din of battle Pullen could not make out what he was saying. She looked back toward the main road and saw Rivera rolling around on the ground, obviously wounded. Mike finally got through on the radio and told Pullen that Rivera, Mack, and Haynes were all wounded. She passed the news on to Nein and then got into her vehicle and pulled it back about 100 meters to get closer to the third HMMWV. Ordunez was still in the turret, and he continued to fire at the field north of the access road as Pullen ran over to help administer aid to Rivera.[38] Writhing in pain, Rivera told Pullen he could not feel his legs. She tried to calm him, "Think about your son. Think about him. Think about anything but this."[39]

The MPs realized they were still taking fire from the rear. One or two insurgents had managed to get into the upper floor of the house on the south side of the road, and they had an open field of fire to shoot at the Americans on the access road. Nein ordered Ordunez to fire the MK19 grenade launcher at the house, but the grenades had no effect. So Cooper and Mike, located at least 175 meters apart, both decided to fire their AT4 rocket launchers at the house. The rockets eliminated the threat, but not before revealing the precariousness of the their position. Thinking they had flanked the enemy by turning up the access road, the MPs had actually placed themselves in the middle of the insurgent forces. Roughly 15 well-armed insurgents were in various positions south of the access road. Had those fighters not been engaged with the northbound convoy throughout the fight, they very well could have done serious damage to the exposed squad.[40]

As Nein took stock of the situation, he began to realize just how small his fighting force had become. At his position, he only had four Soldiers and one vehicle. Only the gunner remained in the second HMMWV, which had pulled back about halfway toward the main road. Mack and Rivera were wounded and out of the fight, and Mike and Pullen were trying to aid their injured squad members. Haynes stayed on the .50-caliber in the third truck, but his wounds kept him from firing at various times during the action. Nein recalled:

> At this point, I'm thinking to myself that we're fighting a platoon-sized or bigger element. . . . At one point, I thought about destroying the Blue Force Tracker [a device in his HMMWV for tracking the locations of friendly forces] because I really thought we were going to be overrun. Because if they had taken over Sergeant Rivera's position, they would have a .50-caliber and I didn't know if we could defend against that.[41]

In the midst of all the confusion of that wide open firefight, a terrible thought entered Nein's mind: "We are all going to die here."[42]

When the MPs had moved back over to the contact side of the south-bound convoy, they had drawn much of the insurgent fire from the two stranded convoys, but that did not stop the action elsewhere on the battlefield. In the northbound convoy, Beck took advantage of the lull created by the MPs to jump out of her truck and instruct the wounded DeLancey to climb in. Beck made her way over to DeLancey's disabled Army truck and found Ricketts face down in the cab, still pinned under the collapsed dashboard. He told her that he was stuck and that he was not going to get out. She grabbed him by the arm and yelled, "There's no way we're leaving you here. On the count of three, you push and I'll pull. Do it for me and yourself. You're going to be OK."[43] Together they managed to free him from the wrecked cab and pull him down to the ground. Exhausted by the effort, Beck helped Ricketts around the front of Hart's truck, and then the contractor came over and helped the injured Soldier the rest of the way. There was no more room in her vehicle, so she instructed Hart to help Ricketts take cover under the civilian truck and radioed back that someone needed to pick up the wounded Soldier on their way out of the kill zone. Beck drove her truck across the median and into the southbound lane, and then proceeded north to the casualty collection point. Another section of the convoy followed, but roughly a quarter of the trucks were still in the kill zone, with their drivers hiding in ditches along the side of the road.[44]

Soldiers from the last two Army trucks in the convoy took the lead in getting the rest of the convoy moving. With the disabled Regulator 2 providing cover fire from the rear of the convoy, two of the 1075th Soldiers, SPC Joshua Birkel and SPC Michael Sharples, dismounted and ran the few hundred meters to Hart's truck, trying to prompt the drivers along the way to return to their vehicles. When they reached Hart, they asked him to put the wounded Ricketts in his truck and drive out to the casualty collection point. Hart complied, and the two Soldiers worked their way back toward their trucks, begging, pleading, and even forcing the civilian drivers back into their vehicles and on the road again. They finally got all the trucks moving, and the northbound convoy began to clear the kill zone.[45]

Before the convoy left, Regulator 3, the final guntruck in the northbound convoy under the command of SGT Rondell Brown, had been receiving heavy enemy fire from the rear of the convoy. Three of their tires had been shot flat within minutes of the outbreak of the fight. Looking for cover, they moved forward on the right side of the convoy vehicles that had not yet left the kill zone. After driving a few hundred meters, they cut back across what was left of their convoy and found themselves approaching the access road. When they arrived at the scene, they found the fight still raging, only now there were at least five HMMWVs on the access road.[46] The various combat elements in both convoys had begun to converge on the main point of action.

It had taken the Soldiers of Stallion 33, the escorts for the southbound convoy, a few minutes to realize what was going on and react to the situation. When the ambush started, Stallion 33A, the lead HMMWV, had pulled out of the kill zone and moved south to the Iraqi checkpoint. The second HMMWV, Stallion 33B, drove past the front of the convoy and tried to get the convoy moving; however, the tractor-trailer that had been hit by an RPG and caught fire was now billowing black smoke over the entire battlefield, and the civilian drivers were too panicked to get back into their trucks. Unsure of what to do next, the Soldiers of Stallion 33 began to hear segments of the fight over the radio. It became clear that there were wounded American Soldiers on the access road, and the MPs could use all the help they could get. Stallion 33B turned around and headed back toward the access road. Stallion 33C, which had been at the rear of the southbound convoy at the beginning of the fight, moved forward and reached the corner of the main route and access road first.

With the bullets still flying everywhere and Pullen and Mike trying to help the wounded Mack and Rivera, the men of Stallion 33C hesitated at first, unsure of where to help. SGT Ricky Burke, the vehicle commander, dismounted and made his way over to Pullen and Mike, who both yelled at him to lay down suppressive fire or help with the wounded. Burke and his driver, SGT Matthew Simpson, helped move Mack to a safer position under cover of the vehicles.[47] Regulator 3 now came on the scene, and vehicle commander Brown helped move Rivera to better cover.[48] Stallion 33B also arrived, and the squad leader, Hammons, and his driver loaded Mack into their vehicle to get him out of the area. As Stallion 33B continued on their way south, they made contact with Stallion 33A returning from the checkpoint. Hammons ordered Stallion 33A to return southward to set up a MEDEVAC point and followed in his vehicle with the wounded Mack. They dropped Mack off at the MEDEVAC point and returned to the access road.[49]

Two hundred meters down the access road, Nein decided the time had come for more decisive action. He had made repeated calls for close air support, but it was still a few minutes away. And, for all he knew, the third truck in his squad was either out of action or about to be, so no help was coming from that direction either. The gunners in all three of his vehicles had eliminated most of the targets out in the field, but at least four insurgents had taken up positions in the trench line on the north side of the access road. Concerned that he had to do something to get his squad out of there alive, Nein thought, "we need to go on the super offensive. We need to start going into the canal system; we need to charge these guys."[50]

From his position on the berm, Nein called out to Hester and Morris that he needed someone with a M203 grenade launcher and then jumped into the trench in front of him. Hester was closer to Nein than Morris, so she jumped in alongside her squad leader.[51] They began to move down the trench system toward the main road in 10-meter rushes, while Morris covered them and the insurgent getaway vehicles along the berm.[52] Nein described what happened next:

> One of the things we always talked about was that if we
> had to go head-to-head with somebody, always try to keep

our body armor square with the bad guy: that way we had the best ballistic protection from our vest. We stayed squared up. I stepped off to the left and she shot two 203s [grenades], but she couldn't get them low enough because they were about 50 meters in front of us at that time. I told her we just had to keep going and so we started throwing grenades and shooting our M4s. She would shoot over my right shoulder while I prepared the grenade to throw it, or I would be shooting while she threw a grenade. I had three grenades when I left that morning. I'd already thrown one. I threw two more in the canal off my vest and she had two on her as well. I threw one of hers and she threw one of hers. Basically, 5 or 10 minutes into the canal system we'd killed the four guys.[53]

It had not been easy, in part because the shorter barreled M4s did not have much stopping power. According to Nein, "There wasn't one guy we shot with our M4s that went down with one hit; most of them had to be shot three or four times before they went down."[54]

As Nein, Hester, and Morris made their way down the trench line toward the main road, the battle began to turn decisively in the Americans' favor. Ordunez and Haynes had kept up their fire on the insurgents in the field and main trench line, but now they found themselves joined by several other gunners at or near the intersection of the trenches. After Nein and Hester had gone into the trench, the gunner in the lead MP vehicle, Cooper, shot the engine blocks of the parked insurgent vehicles. He noticed that the action was still hot back toward the main road, so he dropped down into the driver's seat of his damaged HMMVW. By some miracle the truck still ran, and Cooper backed it up and got back into the fight.[55] At the same time, the Stallion crews still on the scene began to fire down the trench line, and the crew of Regulator 3 also opened fire on the field and trenches.[56] The accumulation of fire, along with the actions of Nein and Hester, devastated what was left of the insurgent force.

At the very end, the trench system carried Nein and Hester into the rest of the Americans' fields of fire. Mike saw them coming and called for everyone to cease fire. One more insurgent popped up and shot a full magazine from his hip at the charging Americans. Nein remembered "seeing the bullets hitting everywhere," and he could not believe he had not been hit.[57] He and Hester took out this last insurgent, and the fire died down in the field. The Palm Sunday Ambush was over.

Mike, Pullen, and the crews of Regulator 3 and Stallion 33B transported the wounded Rivera and Haynes and the driver of Regulator 2, who they picked up as they passed the northbound convoy, to the MEDEVAC point.[58] Air support, the MP company commander (Lindner), and multiple other vehicles arrived on the scene. Lindner took over the efforts to police the area.[59]

The northbound convoy had lost several vehicles in the ambush and took several casualties but incurred no fatalities. The southbound convoy directly in front of the main insurgent force had not been quite so lucky. Multiple trucks were damaged beyond repair and could not continue, and three civilian drivers had died in the fight. The Army casualties, including Rivera, Mack, Ricketts, DeLancey, Graff, Harris, and Hubbard, all survived their wounds.

Patrols through the insurgent positions found only shell casings south of the access road, including some in the two-story house, where the smaller group of insurgents had been during the fight. If any of the enemy in that area had been killed or wounded, the insurgents had taken the casualties with them when they escaped.[60] The trenches and field north of the access road were a different story. Insurgent bodies were scattered all over the field, many of them carrying handcuffs—most likely to be used in taking prisoners from the convoy. Twenty-four insurgents were killed on the scene, nine were wounded (two of whom later died from their wounds), and one was captured unharmed. Over 30 automatic weapons, multiple RPG tubes and rockets, thousands of rounds of ammunition, and 40 hand grenades littered the area.[61]

Eventually, Nein, Hester, and Mike would receive the Silver Star for their actions in the fight. Cooper, Haynes, and Pullen would receive the Bronze Star, and Morris and Ordunez would receive the Army Commendation Medal with Valor distinction (ARCOM-V). Three Soldiers from the Stallion element would also receive the ARCOM-V. From the 1075th, Beck, DeLancey, Birkel, and Sharples would receive the Bronze Star, and Graff would receive the ARCOM-V.

But all that was a few months later. On the afternoon of Palm Sunday 2005, the newly minted veterans of one of the largest and most complex ambushes in the Iraq War had to get back to work. Even as recently arrived units policed the battlefield, the uninjured Soldiers from the fight repaired their damaged vehicles and got back on the road. The shaken convoys pulled together and continued on their way to their ultimate objectives, leaving behind the burned-out husks of trucks destroyed in the battle. The troops had a job to do; they had to keep the trucks running. For the Soldiers of the Palm Sunday ambush, the war went on.

Notes

1. For background on US Army convoy operations and convoy operations in Iraq, see Steve Harding, "Movement Masters," *Soldiers* 60 (April 2005) : 8–17; Christopher Prawdzik, "Highways Through Hell," *National Guard* 59 (June 2005) : 26–29; and Richard E. Killblane, *Circle the Wagons: The History of US Army Convoy Security*, Global War on Terrorism Occasional Paper 13 (Fort Leavenworth, KS: Combat Studies Institute Press, 2005).

2. SSG Timothy F. Nein, interview by author, 28 June 2006, digital recording, Fort Leavenworth, KS; CPT Lawrence Joiner, phone interview by author, 27 July 2006.

3. The area generally was a hotspot for the insurgency in the spring of 2005. See "Enclosure A: Eastern Route Threat Assessment, 16 March 2005," in Michael A. Migliara, "AAR Comments on 20 March 05 Ambush on ASR Detroit," 29 March 2005.

4. The main highway ran generally in a north-south route, but at the point of contact, the lanes ran on a compass from northwest to southeast. The access road ran linear southwest off the main road. For the purposes of this study, the route lanes are described as southbound and northbound, with the access road to the west.

5. The 1075th was a Nebraska National Guard Unit. For background on them, see Kevin Hynes, "Under Fire," *Prairie Soldier* 56 (February 2006) : 10–13. The 518th was a provisional company that had been created out of volunteers from Active Duty, National Guard, and Army Reserve units at the behest of CPT Robert Landry in the spring of 2004 to help provide convoy security. See Harding, "Movement Matters," 13; Stephanie Heinatz, "Gun Trucks Offer Safety on Deadly Routes," *Hampton Roads Daily Press*, 26 September 2004, online at <www.dailypress.com>, accessed 9 May 2006; Harry Levins, "To Protect Convoys in Iraq, Captain Built Unit from Scratch," *St. Louis Post Dispatch*, 22 January 2005, online at <www.stltoday.com>, accessed 30 May 2006; and Brian Trapp, "Not Your Typical Escort Service," *Desert Voice* 26 (8 June 2005) : 5.

6. Hynes, "Under Fire," 13.

7. The 623d FA Regiment and 617th MP Company were Kentucky National Guard units.

8. SGT Dustin Morris, interview by author, 19 July 2006, digital recording, Fort Leavenworth, KS.

9. Nein interview; Morris interview; SPC Ashley Pullen, interview by author, 16 August 2006, digital recording, Fort Leavenworth, KS; Donna Miles, "Guard Unit Credits Training in Overcoming 27 Insurgents," American Forces Information Service, 22 March 2005, online at <www.dod.mil/news>, accessed 5 June 2006.

10. William P. Young, DA Form 2823, Sworn Statement, 21 March 2005; James R. Baker, DA Form 2823, Sworn Statement, 21 March 2005; Patrick T. Malone, DA Form 2823, Sworn Statement, 21 March 2005.

11. CPT Eric S. Minor, "Historical Summary of 20 MAR 05 Ambush on ASR

Detroit," 27 March 2005; SPC Kevin R. Vogel, DA Form 2823, Sworn Statement, 21 March 2005; SFC Rickie Hammons, DA Form 2823, Sworn Statement, 21 March 2005; SPC Richard S. Saylor, DA Form 2823, Sworn Statement, 21 March 2005.

12. SGT Matthew T. Simpson, DA Form 2823, Sworn Statement, 21 March 2005; SGT Ricky Burke, DA Form 2823, Sworn Statement, 21 March 2005; SPC Kirby L. Gregory, DA Form 2823, Sworn Statement, 21 March 2005.

13. Untitled video, filmed by PFC Jairo Torres, 20 March 2005; Regulator 1, 518th Guntruck Company Audio After Action Review, 26 March 2005.

14. Quoted in Hynes, "Under Fire," 14.

15. Ibid., 14; Kevin Hynes, "Courage Under Fire," *Prairie Soldier*, 56 (April 2006) : 13.

16. Charles Gilkey, "Convoy 678N Engagement Narrative"; Hynes, "Under Fire," 15; Henry J. Cordes, "Nebraska Guard Unit Recalls Ambush in Iraq," *Omaha World-Herald*, 29 May 2005, online at <http://www.omaha.com/>, accessed 30 May 2006.

17. Regulator 2, 518th Guntruck Company Audio After Action Review, 26 March 2005.

18. Hynes, "Courage Under Fire," 15.

19. Cordes, "Nebraska Guard Unit"; Hynes, "Under Fire," 15; Gilkey, "Convoy 678N Engagement."

20. Ron Hart, telephone interview by Richard Kilblane, 12 May 2006; Hynes, "Courage Under Fire," 16.

21. Hynes, "Courage Under Fire," 14–15.

22. Cordes, "Nebraska Guard Unit."

23. Hynes, "Under Fire," 15.

24. Regulator 1, 518th Guntruck Company, After Action Review, 26 March 2005.

25. Untitled video provided by LT Charles Gilkey, unidentified videographer, 20 March 2005, in author's possession.

26. Untitled insurgent video, unidentified videographer, 20 March 2005, Digital Video and Imagery Distribution System (DVIDS), online at <http//:www.dvidshub.net>, accessed 1 June 2006.

27. Michael A. Migliara, "AAR Comments on 20 March 05 Ambush on ASR Detroit," 29 March 2005; Jeremy D. Crisp, "It Was Supposed to be Another Routine Mission in Iraq," Third Army/ARCENT/CFLCC, 23 March 2003, online at <www.arcent.army.mil/news>, accessed 5 June 2006.

28. SPC Casey M. Cooper, DA Form 2823, Sworn Statement, 21 March 2005.

29. SGT Leigh Ann Hester, DA Form 2823, Sworn Statement, 21 March 2005; Nein interview; "Guard Unit Ambushed in Iraq," *Macomb Daily*, 22 March 2005, online at <www.macombdaily.com/stories>, accessed 5 June 2006.

30. SPC Ashley Pullen, video interview, MP Interviews After Insurgent Ambush, n.d., Digital Video and Imagery Distribution System (DVIDS), online at <http//:www.dvidshub.net>, accessed 1 June 2006.

31. Pullen interview.

32. Jared Nelson, "Princeton Soldier Involved in Iraqi Firefight," *Princeton Times Leader*, 27 March 2005, online at <www.timesleader.net/articles/stories/public>, accessed 5 June 2006.

33. Nein interview.

34. Nein interview; SSG Timothy F. Nein, DA Form 2823, Sworn Statement, 21 March 2005; Hester Sworn Statement; Morris interview; Pullen interview.

35. SPC Jason L. Mike, DA Form 2823, Sworn Statement, 20 March 2005.

36. Ibid.

37. SGT Jesse Ordunez, interview by author, 18 July 2006, digital recording, Fort Leavenworth, KS; SPC Jesse Ordunez, DA Form 2823, Sworn Statement, 6 August 2005.

38. Mike Sworn Statement; Pullen interview; SPC Ashley J. Pullen, DA Form 2823, Sworn Statement, 24 March 2005.

39. Steve Fainaru, "Silver Stars Affirm One Unit's Mettle," *Washington Post*, 26 June 2005, A1; Pullen interview.

40. Nein interview; Nein Sworn Statement; Ordunez Sworn Statement; Cooper Sworn Statement; Mike Sworn Statement.

41. Nein interview.

42. Ibid.

43. Cordes, "Nebraska Guard"; Gilkey, "Convoy 678N Engagement"; Hart interview.

44. Hynes, "Courage Under Fire," 16.

45. Kevin Hynes, "Forgotten," *Prairie Soldier* 56 (June 2006) : 13–17; Gilkey, "Convoy 678N Engagement."

46. Regulator 3, 518th Guntruck Company Audio After Action Review, 26 March 2005; Hynes, "Courage Under Fire," 14; Gilkey, "Convoy 678N Engagement."

47. "Historical Summary on 20 MAR 05 Ambush"; Simpson Sworn Statement; Burke Sworn Statement; Mike Sworn Statement; Pullen Sworn Statement; Pullen interview.

48. Pullen interview.

49. Hammons Sworn Statement.

50. Nein interview.

51. Morris interview; Hester Sworn Statement.

52. Hester Sworn Statement.

53. Nein interview.

54. Ibid.

55. Cooper Sworn Statement.

56. Regulator 3 Audio After Action Review; Mike Sworn Statement.

57. Nein interview.

58. Mike Sworn Statement; Pullen Sworn Statement; Hammons Sworn Statement; "Historical Summary of the 20 MAR 05 Ambush"; Regulator 2 Audio After Action Review.

59. Convoy Incident Report, Blue-3 Spot Report, 18th Military Police Bde, 20 March 2005; Bob Haskell, "Kentucky Soldiers Turn the Tables on Heavily-Armed Insurgents," *On Guard* (May 2005), online at <www.ngb.army.mil/onguard>, accessed 5 June 2006.

60. "Historical Summary on 20 MAR 05 Ambush"; Gilkey, "Convoy 678N Engagement"; Ordunez interview; Nein interview.

61. CPT Todd Lindner, "AAR 20 Mar 2005 Ambush, 617th MP Company."

Operation TRAFFIC STOP:
1-64th Armor in Baghdad, 13 July 2005

by

LTC Kevin E. Kennedy

Following the removal of the Saddam Hussein regime in 2003, American and Coalition forces sought to establish a stable, prosperous, and democratic Iraq. The 1st Battalion, 64th Armor Regiment (1-64 AR) deployed for a second time to Iraq in February 2005 as part of the third overall rotation of troops to Operation IRAQI FREEDOM. The battalion, like its parent unit the 2d Brigade Combat Team of the 3d Infantry Division (Mechanized), had gained fame in the division's historic thrust along the Euphrates River and subsequent armored raids, the so-called "Thunder Runs," into Baghdad during the spring of 2003. Nicknamed "Desert Rogues," the battalion served its second 1-year tour in the capital city of Baghdad. The mission of 1-64 AR was to promote stability and security; to improve the Iraqi security forces; to assist the Iraq people and government in bringing about a stable, legitimate government; and to support economic development.[1]

The 1-64 AR deployed as a combined arms battalion under the Army's new modular concept. Under this organization, the battalion was permanently organized with two infantry companies (A and B Companies), two tank companies (C and D Companies), a mechanized engineer company (E Company), a forward support company employed in a direct support mode (F Company), and a headquarters company. The headquarters company (HHC) consisted of a motorized scout platoon, a mechanized mortar platoon, and a medical platoon. Additionally, the battalion contained several attachments: a section of military working dogs, a tactical human intelligence team, and a civil affairs team. The overall strength of the unit was 817 Soldiers out of an authorized strength of 926.[2]

When the unit reorganized as a combined arms battalion, it drew personnel and equipment from across the division. For the most part, entire companies came to the battalion, with the exception of B Company. Created from the ground up, this company did not have any of its authorized M2 Bradley Infantry Fighting Vehicles at the time of deployment. The company, along with the rest of the battalion, would draw M1114 uparmored high-mobility multipurpose wheeled vehicles (HMMWVs) in the theater of operations for its subsequent employment in Iraq. During the course of the deployment, B Company fielded a number of Bradleys, though it never reached its authorized strength while in Iraq.[3] The rest of the battalion's maneuver units were fully equipped with two companies of M1 Abrams tanks and one company of Bradleys. Thus, 1-64 AR was adequately though not fully equipped for its mission in Iraq.

The Desert Rogues assumed responsibility for an area in eastern Baghdad from the 1st Battalion, 12th Cavalry Regiment, 1st Cavalry Division, and dubbed it Area of Operations (AO) ROGUE. This area was mainly the Tisa Nissan District, also known as Nine Nissan, Baghdad Jadeeda, and New Baghdad (see map 6). It is located east of the Tigris River and borders the Thawra District (better known as Sadr City) in the west and the Diyala River in the east. The battalion subdivided the AO into six zones and assigned responsibility for each to a company. Two forward operating bases (FOBs) were located within AO ROGUE. The entire battalion was housed at FOB RUSTAMIYAH, while the 2d Brigade Combat Team (BCT) headquarters and the 1st Battalion, 9th Field Artillery Regiment occupied FOB LOYALTY. A third FOB was located just outside AO ROGUE's northern boundary at FOB HOPE and the 3d Battalion, 15th Infantry Regiment occupied it; for the first 3 months, this area fell in AO ROGUE. Because of the three FOBs in relatively close proximity to each other, four main supply routes (MSRs) transited AO ROGUE. Three of these MSRs were major city boulevards comparable to any major thoroughfare in a large US city, while the fourth MSR was a six-lane divided highway comparable to an American interstate highway. All of these routes were intersected by smaller streets and bisected the many residential neighborhoods that characterize Baghdad. Over the course of the deployment, 1-64 AR would devote much of its time and effort to securing these lines of communication. Overall, AO ROGUE was urban and encompassed about 40 square kilometers with a population of 1.6 million people.[4]

AO ROGUE was representative of many areas of Baghdad in its religious and ethnic diversity, mixture of neighborhoods, and dense urban population. In terms of religion, 1-64 AR patrolled areas populated by Christians, Sunnis, Shias, and Palestinians. The Christian neighborhoods were generally affluent, clean, and presented few problems for the Coalition. LTC Kevin Farrell, the 1-64 AR commander, compared the Christian area in Nine Nissan to a neighborhood one might encounter in Florida with manicured lawns, palm trees, and clean streets.[5] Indeed, even Shias and Sunnis largely respected the Christian population, and there was very little hostility directed against it. Sunnis occupied several small zones of AO ROGUE. The largest concentration of Sunnis was in an affluent neighborhood in the southwest corner of the AO. Former regime generals

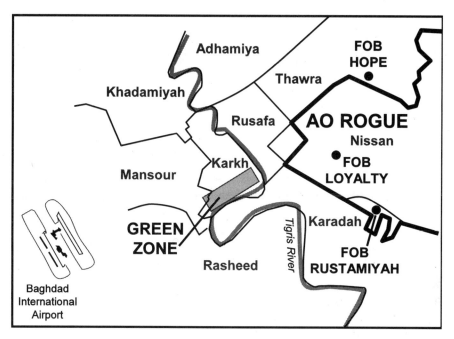

Map 6. AO ROGUE.

and other retired high-ranking officials lived in this area. During its time in Nine Nissan, the Desert Rogues did not encounter any overt resistance from the Sunni areas, though the inhabitants were usually cold and mistrustful toward the presence of Coalition forces. Palestinians occupied a small neighborhood in the center of AO ROGUE. When Saddam Hussein was in power, the Palestinians were in favor as Saddam attempted to show his Pan Arab allegiance and disdain for Israel. However, with the end of the Saddam regime, the Palestinian group in Nine Nissan became what Farrell described as "the new low man on the totem pole and was blamed for all bad things that occurred in the area."[6] Shias made up about 70 percent of the population in AO ROGUE, and most lived in densely packed neighborhoods in abject squalor.[7] Some of the poorest neighborhoods in Baghdad were located within the Nine Nissan District. Crime in these areas ran rampant while there was little to no sewage system, electricity, running water, or trash collection. Surprisingly, the Desert Rogues discovered that the Sunni and Shia animosity was not as striking as they initially expected. Though there was some sectarian violence in parts of the area of operations, differences among the population were characterized more by wealth than religious affiliation.[8]

The enemy facing 1-64 AR was ill defined. Farrell described one of the biggest challenges throughout the deployment as identifying the enemy and determining his motivations and allegiances.[9] The battalion faced what it believed to be an assortment of Anti-Iraqi Forces (AIFs) varying from Sunni groups (Ansar al Sunnah, al-Qaeda in Iraq, etc.), Shia groups (First Fraternity of Fadhil Abd Al Abbas, Mahdi Militia, etc.), and several other terrorist organizations consisting of foreign fighters and suspected foreign operatives. Though not a direct threat to Coalition forces, criminal organizations destabilized Iraqi society through kidnappings for ransom, drug trafficking, and gun running.

The enemy directly attacked 1-64 AR and other Coalition forces through a variety of means: improvised explosive devices (IEDs), small arms fire, vehicle-borne improvised explosive devices (VBIEDs), and indirect fire attacks. All methods were potentially effective because they were simple and required few people to execute the attack. In addition, the dense nature of the terrain allowed individuals to simply blend into the crowd. The other advantage the area of operations afforded the enemy was ready-made engagement areas in the form of MSRs. Coalition forces routinely traversed the major roads, traveling between FOBs, logistics hubs, and the International (Green) Zone just to the west of AO ROGUE. While transiting these major thoroughfares, vehicular convoys became the target of choice for the various AIF groups and represented the largest proportion of attacks on Coalition forces in the area.[10] In AO ROGUE the enemy's preferred method of attack involved IEDs, both roadside bombs and vehicle-borne devices. The most common alternate method of attack was with small arms fire, normally directed at checkpoints or dismounted Soldiers.

As part of its overall mission in Iraq, 1-64 AR conducted numerous offensive operations to isolate and neutralize AIF elements. From early March to mid-July 2005, the battalion conducted 10 major operations. These operations occurred throughout the AO—in the residential neighborhoods, the business districts, and along the MSRs. Operations were routinely conducted with Iraqi security forces as part of the effort to train Iraqis to assume responsibility for their own security. These missions ranged widely in purpose: searches for IED materials and IED fabricating equipment, detention of suspected AIF elements, interdiction of the flow of contraband materials through the area, and election support preparation. Throughout all of these missions, the Desert Rogue Soldiers engaged the population to gain intelligence and to build rapport with the citizens. The operations had mixed results, as the battalion never had a defining moment in which it uncovered a base of opposition. However, the battalion had individual successes, such as the discovery of a VBIED factory during a Joint Iraqi Intervention Force cordon and search. It also met some success in disrupting the flow of illegal weapons and materials transiting the area.

The effort to gain intelligence from the population was frustrating. The Desert Rogue Soldiers scoured the different neighborhoods of the AO and found that the population was generally receptive to their presence. Nevertheless, when asked about who was responsible for attacks on Coalition forces, the citizens would reply that they did not know or that the insurgents came from far away.[11] Battalion personnel assumed initially that the insurgent activities came from the local populace and that the citizens had complete situational awareness of their neighborhoods. Gradually, through analysis, the battalion's leaders began to question those assumptions. First, the unit realized that the oppressive Saddam regime had inculcated into the minds of Iraqis that they should not know too much about their surroundings. To the individual Iraqi, that might mean knowing some neighbors on the block or street, but anything beyond that could arouse suspicion. Simply knowing someone who was up to no good would be enough to make an innocent citizen guilty by association. Therefore, the average citizen might be aware of outsiders coming to his neighborhood to shoot a mortar or emplace a bomb, but he was very hesitant to learn anything more; in Iraq one minded his own business or suffered the consequences for knowing too much.

Further analysis confirmed that the enemy did not use neighborhoods as a base from which to launch strikes against the Coalition. An assessment of enemy direct action incidents during the period from March to June 2005 showed that they were the types of attacks that could be carried out by small cells. The attacks were never more than a single event—a couple of mortar rounds or rockets, a bomb, or small arms fire. In not using the neighborhoods that overlooked engagement areas, the enemy could not combine engagement methods into a complex ambush. This trend could have been deliberate, indicating that the resistance in the area was not large enough to mobilize the necessary resources, or it could have been by necessity, indicating that the local citizenry did not support such anti-Coalition activities. Through this pattern analysis, population feedback, and lack of illegal materials found in the area, the battalion concluded that the enemy attacks along the MSRs originated from outside AO ROGUE.[12]

Route security became the main and most critical day-to-day mission for 1-64 AR as attacks along the MSRs of AO ROGUE increased during the early summer of 2005.[13] The dilemma of how best to secure the MSRs confronted Farrell. He considered a number of options, including several innovative approaches. The first option was to increase the number of route security patrols. The battalion had previously devoted seven patrols per day to protect the different MSRs. These patrols departed at different times daily and covered different segments of the MSRs in random patterns to keep the enemy off balance. Farrell could increase the number and frequency of these patrols, but that would require more manpower and could detract from other operational requirements in the rest of the AO. Another option was to establish permanent traffic control points (TCPs) at the most frequently targeted areas. Unfortunately, this course of action would drain manpower and also present a fixed target for the enemy. Various measures could be taken to mitigate the force protection risk at the TCPs, and the Iraqi Security Forces (ISF) could be enlisted to augment the effort along the MSRs, but Farrell considered these measures less than optimal. Still another option available to the battalion was employing cameras in problem areas. This alternative would be difficult to pursue because of the cost of the necessary surveillance equipment, the associated maintenance and replacement expenses, and the requirement to maintain a force on constant alert to act on enemy activities. A possible refinement of this course of action would be the employment of dummy surveillance cameras as deterrents, which would reduce the cost. Farrell also considered another innovative approach, operations that targeted a stretch of road during morning or evening rush hour. This undertaking would close a section of road, entrapping cars on it, for a detailed search of every motor vehicle within the cordon. Such an operation could interrupt the flow of contraband materials, catch illegal traffickers and insurgents, and interrupt AIF activity along the designated MSR. An operation of this type could be conducted at the company or battalion level, depending on the magnitude of the search. Finally, Farrell could choose a combination of options to combat the enemy's actions.

*   *   *

On 13 July, 1-64 AR conducted Operation TRAFFIC STOP, a battalion-level operation to halt traffic along a stretch of road and systematically search every vehicle (see map 7). This operation sprang from Farrell's decision to try something new to secure the MSRs, remain unpredictable in the face of the enemy, yet continue normal ongoing route security patrols and TCPs. Farrell's intent was to interdict AIF cells that used the roads to transport illegal items, such as weapons, ammunition, and bomb-making materials. Simultaneously, the operation would clear the road for a short time, display the Coalition's fighting spirit, and demonstrate to the Iraqi people the Coalition's commitment to securing and stabilizing their country.[14]

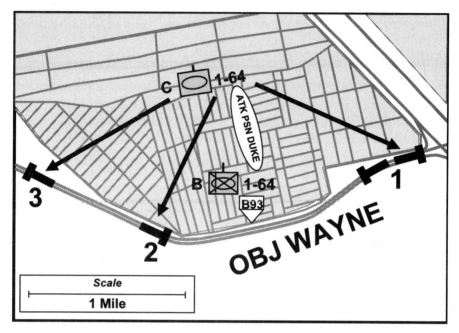

Map 7. Operation TRAFFIC STOP.

The targeted area for Operation TRAFFIC STOP was a six-lane highway that had previously been the site of attacks on Coalition forces. It transited a portion of AO ROGUE and was connected to other large thoroughfares in the region. The battalion could close a 2.5-mile section of the road at two major interchanges and effectively reroute traffic to the other highways without completely snarling traffic throughout the region. Because vehicles caught within the cordon could not easily exit the road, fewer forces would be required to seal the objective area. On one side of the targeted highway was a quiet neighborhood and on the other side was relatively open terrain. The residential district would provide a good attack position next to but separated from the highway and would not arouse suspicion of the impending search. However, the unit operating in the neighborhood would have to commit some combat power to cordon the highway from the residential area. The open ground on the south side of the road offered no easy access to the highway and mounted weapon systems could effectively cover it, thus preventing an attack from the south and denying its use as an escape route. Compared to other thoroughfares throughout the region, this stretch of highway offered the best location for 1-64 AR to test Farrell's new tactic.

The concept of the operation involved using two companies, B and C, to encircle traffic on the designated stretch of highway, divert other vehicles away from it, and clear the vehicles within the cordon. The operation was to be accomplished in five sequential steps: task reorganization, establishment of Attack Position DUKE, establishment of blocking positions, clearance of vehicles on Objective WAYNE, and movement back to FOB RUSTAMIYAH. For the duration of the operation, both companies would revert to pure organizational status the day prior to the mission. Company B, led by CPT Craig Stucker, would be organized solely as infantry and equipped primarily with M1114 HMMWVs, with one platoon employing both M1114s and three M2A2ODS Bradleys. Additionally, the company would gain two teams of MWDs to assist in the systematic search of vehicles. Company C, under CPT William Coryell, would commit all three of its M1 tank platoons, a tactical psychological operations team (TPT), and three M9 Armored Combat Earthmovers (ACEs) to establish roadblocks. Farrell would be present throughout the operation, and the remaining units of the battalion would continue their normal operations throughout the rest of AO ROGUE.

To establish Attack Position DUKE, B Company would depart the FOB at 0800 on 13 July. The company would move by platoon along multiple routes to minimize the signature of the unit moving into place. The company would consolidate loosely at Attack Position DUKE, a series of residential streets that afforded numerous avenues to the objective. B Company would halt for a short time at DUKE and wait for the signal to move forward, through the residential area, and on to Objective WAYNE. Once on the objective, the company would systematically search every vehicle along a 1.5-mile segment of road within the 2.5-mile section of targeted highway.

Company C would depart the FOB at 0915 on 13 July to establish three blocking positions. Blocking Position 1 would be located on the east side of the objective, near a major road intersection, to prevent westbound traffic from backing up. Blocking Position 3 would be located on the west side of the objective and would halt traffic approaching from that direction. Only the northern, westbound, lane of traffic was to be searched. Traffic on the southern, eastbound, lane could exit the objective area after Blocking Position 3 was in place. Blocking Position 2 would halt westward traffic along that northern lane. Once all traffic was halted with Blocking Positions 1 and 3 operational, C Company would employ a roving patrol with a loudspeaker team to address the masses caught within the objective. The TPT would instruct the vehicle occupants to shut down their vehicles; open all doors, trunks, and hoods; and move to the empty southern lane of the divided highway. Once all the Iraqis had complied with these instructions, C Company would signal B Company that the objective was prepared for searching.

On receiving the signal, Stucker planned to approach the objective through the residential area and establish blocking positions where residential streets led toward Objective WAYNE, thus forming a cordon between the objective and the residential area. Next, the company would conduct a dismounted search of all vehicles on the objective between Blocking Positions 2 and 1. The company would search a group of vehicles, mark them as clear, and move on to the next group of vehicles. Once cleared, the vehicles could depart the objective. Anything identified as contraband would be seized and the vehicle occupants detained for further questioning. B Company would continue this process until all vehicles had been searched. On clearing the entire objective, the company would withdraw through Attack Position DUKE to FOB RUSTAMIYAH. Once B Company departed Objective Wayne, C Company would collapse its blocking positions and also return to the FOB.

The battalion issued the operations order for the mission on 10 July at 1700. The company commanders conducted a backbrief for Farrell on 12 July at 1400, using the map rehearsal technique. At this stage of the deployment, the battalion had been conducting continuous operations for 4 months and a full-dress rehearsal was not necessary. Everything that the companies were called on to execute had been conducted numerous times before and had become routine.[15] As is the nature of continuous operations, parallel planning between the companies and the battalion staff had become the norm. So, Stucker and Coryell knew of the upcoming mission well before the battalion order was issued. Both company commanders issued their operations orders to platoon and squad leaders and followed the battalion model of a backbrief type rehearsal using the map technique.

On the day of execution, the operation began smoothly. Company B's platoons departed the FOB sequentially, beginning at 0800. By 0930, the company was consolidated on Attack Position DUKE. Company C's platoons began their individual movements to their assigned blocking positions at 0845. By 0936, all three blocking positions were operational and the TPT began its loudspeaker broadcasts to the 300 vehicles in the cordon.[16] At 0947, C Company began a mounted inspection of the 1.5-mile long objective to ensure that all Iraqi citizens were away from their vehicles and that the objective was clear for B Company to begin its dismounted search.

At 1000, C Company cleared the objective and B Company began its movement through the residential area between Attack Position DUKE and Objective WAYNE. The company moved along multiple avenues and established blocking positions at points where side streets intersected a larger street that bordered the residential area and paralleled the objective. With this cordon in place, B Company began its detailed search of the vehicles within Objective WAYNE. As planned, Stucker rotated his second and third platoons across the objective and systematically searched every vehicle from west to east. The rotation of platoons through the objective accomplished two purposes for the company. It helped to mitigate the sniper threat by minimizing the exposure of each platoon on the objective and ensured that the Soldiers and dog teams searching the objective remained fresh. During the planning for this operation, both the battalion planning staff and Stucker believed that the enemy's most dangerous course of action against B Company was sniper fire.[17]

By rotating platoons on Objective WAYNE, the company constantly changed its posture in front of the enemy. As each platoon searched a certain number of vehicles, it withdrew from the objective, drove down residential side streets, and emerged from the neighborhood further down the objective at a predetermined point to resume its search. At the company level, these rotations were simply a "leapfrogging" of platoons across the objective through the relatively safe urban area. This technique was additionally beneficial for the dog teams. Though early in the day, the temperature in Baghdad that day was already approaching 100 degrees Fahrenheit. Military working dogs must have breaks to remain sharp, and in the extreme heat of Iraq, the necessity to keep the dogs cool becomes critical. Leapfrogging platoons through the neighborhood gave the dogs the respite they needed.

As the search proceeded, the Soldiers found few illegal items. The detailed search of each vehicle comprised visual means, explosives detecting equipment, and the working dogs. The Soldiers found some seemingly suspicious tools, those belonging to a refrigerator repairman, but not the explosives, illegal weapons, munitions, or other contraband material the operation sought to discover. Yet, the operation gained some intangible success in winning support from the local population. One might expect the vehicle occupants to feel inconvenienced and perhaps annoyed at being stopped during the morning rush hour and made to stand on the side of the road in the growing heat. Instead, the leaders of 1-64 AR commented that the Iraqis were very receptive to the mass search and were generally appreciative of the effort.[18] This sentiment speaks highly of the battalion's information operations themes and messages, the ability of the TPT to articulate them, and the professional treatment the Soldiers bestowed on the Iraqis cordoned on Objective WAYNE.

In the neighborhood adjacent to the highway, local inhabitants, consisting mostly of children, gathered around the B Company Soldiers manning the TCPs. The presence of civilians during operations in a city of over 6 million occupants is commonplace. Children often flock to Soldiers, who are well known for their kindness and generosity in giving candy, and the like, to them. Soldiers become accustomed to herds of children shadowing them during routine operations. In fact, the presence of children is normally a positive omen as attacks against Coalition forces rarely occur around children. The presence of children could allow Soldiers in certain situations to relax their vigilance somewhat. The fact that children so freely approached the Desert Rogues spoke highly of the relationship between the Soldiers and the local citizens in this neighborhood.

After searching the objective for just over 30 minutes, B Company was nearing the completion of its mission. Suddenly, at 1036, an explosion shattered the calm of what had been a smooth operation. A large plume of black smoke rose from one of B Company's positions, Checkpoint (CP) B93, at the edge of the residential area and Objective WAYNE. A suicide bomber with a VBIED had driven through the residential neighborhood, approached the checkpoint, and detonated his explosives near the M1114 HMMWV positioned there. The blast killed SPC Benyahmin B. Yahudah and wounded two other Soldiers.[19] Yahudah was a highly regarded 24-year-old medic from Bogart, Georgia, whose loss was devastating to B Company and the battalion as a whole. At the time of the blast, Yahudah was outside the protection of the uparmored vehicle and in the midst of a crowd of local residents. Along with Yahudah, the blast killed approximately 29 innocent Iraqi citizens, the vast majority of whom were children. The site was chaotic, with two houses on fire and casualties littering the scene. Soldiers flocked to the location to assist the wounded and to secure the area. The battalion immediately began evacuating casualties—Soldiers and civilians alike. At 1050, the first vehicles arrived at the battalion aid station in FOB RUSTAMIYAH.

At the blast location, crowds formed as relatives looked for their loved ones and other residents gathered to determine what had happened. In a short time, the crowd became increasingly agitated. Farrell, who had arrived on the scene in a matter of minutes, immediately called for Iraqi police and firefighter support. They responded without delay, and the scene was transferred to Iraqi authority within 15 minutes after the explosion. With the operation nearing the end, Farrell gave the order to withdraw from the objective and return to the FOB.

That night, various press sources bombarded Farrell with phone calls.

Though the media did not descend on the scene of the attack, a non-US source reported the incident before the Army Public Affairs Office could issue a statement. The initial account reported that 27 people died, most of them children, as US troops handed out candy and toys.[20] The article misinterpreted the nature of the mission and created a negative impression of the operation in the minds of many of the local inhabitants. The article suggested that the American mission that day was to pass out candy and toys to children; there was never any mention of the effort to stem the flow of weapons and other illegal items. Numerous residents believed that the presence of the Americans created a lucrative target that the AIF could not resist. It was, therefore, the fault of the Americans, through their very presence, that caused the attack.[21] The press release from the Multinational Force–Iraq Public Affairs Office did little to assuage this sentiment by stating that the incident was under investigation.[22] Through his conversations with the media, Farrell attempted to tell his side of the story but was largely unsuccessful.

In the months that followed, the battalion's relationship with the neighborhood was quite difficult; it was as if the battalion was starting over again to win the trust of the Iraqi people. Through an intense public affairs campaign at the battalion level, over time and with great effort relations improved as residents realized that the Desert Rogues were sincerely interested in their well-being. No group ever claimed responsibility for the bombing. Al-Qaeda in Iraq outwardly denied it was involved. There were no further large-scale attacks in this particular neighborhood during the rest of 1-64 AR's tour in Iraq. Some residents still squarely placed the blame on Musab al-Zarqawi, while others continued to blame the Coalition. What is certain is that in an instant an operation designed to promote stability and security had unforeseen consequences for the overall battalion mission.

After the conclusion of the operation, Farrell led an after action review to determine what went right, what went wrong, and why, to improve the battalion's future performance. A number of things had gone very well. The use of the TPT was instrumental in controlling the crowd on Objective WAYNE. From the outset of the operation, when C Company first established Blocking Position 2, the TPT began broadcasting instructions to direct the citizens on the objective. There were well over 300 people within the battalion's cordon, and throughout the operation the crowd remained orderly. A measure of effectiveness for the TPT was that C Company did not have to take any extraordinary measures to control the throng of people at any time.

The battalion's search techniques were particularly effective. Coryell's plan to conduct a mounted search to clear the objective of Iraqi citizens made B Company's dismounted search that much easier. The added benefit of C Company's mounted search was that it enabled the battalion to identify any suspicious and potentially dangerous vehicles within the cordon. Farrell later remarked that a thorough mounted search could render a dismounted search unnecessary.[23] B Company conducted the dismounted search thoroughly and expeditiously. Stucker's plan to mark vehicles, rotate platoons, and monitor progress of the search as it moved eastward was well synchronized within the company and was carried out efficiently. The accomplishment speaks for itself; the company was able to search individually 300 vehicles in just under an hour.

The battalion's planning and preparation for Operation TRAFFIC STOP manifested itself on the objective. Parallel planning enabled multiple echelons to prepare for the mission simultaneously in a short period of time. The ability to conduct daily missions and to save time is crucial in a place like Baghdad where units do not have the luxury of pausing current operations to build up for a large operation. Adopting the task organization for the mission early, and the subsequent integration of the TPT and MWD teams into the plan, further enhanced the planning process. The map rehearsals at the battalion and company levels were appropriate for the mission. The familiarity the battalion gained from operating in Baghdad for the better part of 3 months enabled each echelon of command to focus on synchronization, more so than having to concentrate on accomplishing new tasks. The result of the battalion's effort was evident on the streets of Baghdad as every element was in the right place at the right time throughout the operation.

Another positive aspect of the operation was the react-to-contact battle drill and casualty evacuation. When the VBIED detonated, Farrell and Stucker arrived at the scene immediately to gain control of the situation. Recognizing the effect of the incident on the local population, Farrell rightfully involved Iraqi security forces and emergency response personnel to take charge of the civilian assistance effort. Meanwhile, Stucker's troops secured the blast site as first aid and casualty evacuation became the paramount concern. This effort speaks for itself as the first wounded personnel arrived at the battalion aid station 13 minutes after the attack.

Farrell and the other leaders of 1-64 AR identified a number of areas in need of improvement. The first one dealt with anticipating enemy actions. Though the battalion did a superior job in preparing for the mission, it failed to focus on evolving threats outside the cordon throughout the course of the operation. The threat at the beginning of the operation was assumed the same threat throughout the mission, sniper fire or a VBIED within the cordon or a VBIED attack against Blocking Position 1 or 3. No one anticipated a VBIED attack against the checkpoints in the residential area, especially since attacks in the neighborhoods had been nonexistent prior to the time of the operation. This misperception explains why CP B93 did not have a marked no penetration line or spike strips to disable vehicles, leaving it vulnerable to the VBIED attack.

Another problem that plagued the battalion, and other units located throughout Iraq, was how to keep civilians away from ongoing operations. Children flock to US Army patrols, whether mounted or dismounted. Outside of a victim's immediate family, no one is more upset about civilian casualties than the Soldier on the ground who witnesses the death and dismemberment firsthand. Following the events of Operation TRAFFIC STOP, Farrell, in an attempt to curb civilians from crowding Soldiers, forbade his Soldiers from giving candy to children until leaving an area.[24] Coryell told the members of the neighborhood advisory council in his area to keep children away from his Soldiers for their own safety. The battalion used traffic cones at all static locations to mark no penetration lines. The Iraqis in AO ROGUE knew what the traffic cones meant and stayed away from them whether mounted or dismounted. This technique was not new for the battalion, but became standard for all checkpoints and traffic control points regardless of their location.

Farrell recognized the need to minimize further the time spent on an objective. The longer Soldiers remain in an exposed position, the easier it becomes for the enemy to target them, mobilize assets, and attack. The battalion believed that there was no consolidated AIF cell in their area, so to gather the necessary people, weapons, and equipment the enemy needed time. One hour had passed from the time C Company emplaced its first blocking position to the VBIED attack. Prior to the operation, the consensus in the battalion was that 1 hour spent on an objective was not too long. The VBIED attack at CP B93 proved this premise false. After Operation TRAFFIC STOP, Farrell limited actions on an objective to 10 minutes.

One of the largest lessons learned from this particular experience was the necessity to consider the impact of the operation on information operations (IO), from the individual family to the neighborhood level in and around the objective. Operation TRAFFIC STOP was conducted with the best of intentions: to interdict the flow of contraband weapons, explosives, and bomb-making materials. The battalion's media themes and messages were very well developed for the objective area. From an IO perspective, the battalion was just as unprepared for a VBIED attack in the neighborhood as CP B93 was tactically. Part of the problem was beyond Farrell's control. Another TPT for B Company's cordon in the neighborhood would have been a definite combat multiplier had it been available, but it was not. Farrell was on the blast site to talk to the media, but the press did not descend on the scene and interviewed no Soldiers. The battalion's crisis management response package (prepackaged pallets of water, building materials, and hallal meals) was inappropriate for the situation that developed. For subsequent missions, the battalion prepared contingency plans for dealing with crowds, developed IO themes and messages for the outlying areas of an operation, and further integrated Iraqi security forces into the scheme of maneuver.

Operation TRAFFIC STOP had points of success, and the battalion learned some very tough lessons. In this sense, the mission was typical of ongoing operations in Iraq during the early years of the 21st century. Units learned by doing, incorporated lessons learned, and moved on to the next mission; the enemy remained innovative, adaptive, and oftentimes uncaring of the local population. 1-64 AR served with distinction for another 6 months in Baghdad. It conducted numerous battalion-level operations, to include election support for two historic national elections. Simultaneously, it improved the infrastructure for the 1.6 million residents of AO ROGUE, trained Iraqi security forces, and secured some of the most dangerous routes in Baghdad on a daily basis. The battalion sustained significant losses through a difficult year in a very challenging environment. In January 2006, the battalion conducted a transition of authority to elements of the 4th Infantry Division. Much work remained for the Soldiers of the 4th Infantry Division, but Nine Nissan was a better place than it had been a year earlier because of the efforts of 1-64 AR.

Notes

1. LTC Kevin Farrell, interview by Operational Leadership Experiences (OLE) Project Team, Combat Studies Institute, digital recording, 11 April 2006. Fort Leavenworth, KS. [Digital recording stored on CD-ROM at Combined Arms Research Library, Fort Leavenworth, KS.]

2. LTC Kevin Farrell, CPT William Coryell, and CPT Craig Stucker, 1-64 Armor, "Operation TRAFFIC STOP: Background Information" (presentation, presented to Combat Studies Institute, Fort Leavenworth, KS, 10 April 2006).

3. Ibid.

4. Ibid.

5. LTC Kevin Farrell, "U.S.—Iraqi Joint Operations" (speech, presented at The 2006 TRADOC/Combat Studies Institute Military History Symposium, Fort Leavenworth, Kansas, 8–10 August 2006).

6. 1-64 Armor, "Operation TRAFFIC STOP: Background Information" (10 April 2006).

7. CPT Craig Stucker, interview by Operational Leadership Experiences (OLE) Project Team, Combat Studies Institute, digital recording, 11 April 2006, Fort Leavenworth, KS. [Digital recording stored on CD-ROM at Combined Arms Research Library, Fort Leavenworth, KS.]

8. 1-64 Armor, "Operation TRAFFIC STOP: Background Information" (10 April 2006).

9. Farrell interview.

10. 1-64 Armor, "Operation TRAFFIC STOP: Background Information" (10 April 2006).

11. CPT William Coryell, interview by Operational Leadership Experiences (OLE) Project Team, Combat Studies Institute, digital recording, 11 April 2006. Fort Leavenworth, KS. [Digital recording stored on CD-ROM at Combined Arms Research Library, Fort Leavenworth, KS.]

12. 1-64 Armor, "Operation TRAFFIC STOP: Background Information" (10 April 2006).

13. Farrell, "U.S.—Iraqi Joint Operations."

14. LTC Kevin Farrell, CPT William Coryell, and CPT Craig Stucker, 1-64 Armor, "Operation TRAFFIC STOP" (presentation, presented to Combat Studies Institute, Fort Leavenworth, KS, 11 April 2006).

15. Ibid.

16. Ibid.

17. Ibid.

18. Ibid.

19. Fort Stewart Public Affairs Office, "Bogart, GA Native Dies in Action," Press Release Number PR05-118, 15 July 2005, online at <http://www.stewart. army.mil/IMA/sites/news/July05/Yahudah.asp>, accessed 29 August 2006.

20. Andy Mosher and Khalid Alsaffar, "Bombing in Iraq Kills Mostly Children," *Washington Post*, 13 July 2005, online at <http://www.washingtonpost.

com/wp-dyn/content/article/2005/07/13/AR2005071300336.html>, accessed 29 August 2006.

21. 1-64 Armor, "Operation TRAFFIC STOP" (11 April 2006).

22. Multinational Forces–Iraq Public Affairs Office, "U.S. Soldier, Iraqi Children Killed in Attack," Press Release Number A050713b, 13 July 2005, online at <http://www.mnf-iraq.com/index.php?option=com_content& task=vie w&id=3737&Itemid=21>, accessed 29 August 2006.

23. 1-64 Armor, "Operation TRAFFIC STOP" (11 April 2006).

24. Ibid.

Punishment in Syahcow, Afghanistan, 25 July 2005

by

Pete Boisson

My guidance to them is to pressure the enemy, pursue
them aggressively, and don't break contact with them.

—LTC Don Bolduc, Commander, 1st
Bn, 3d SF Group, "Desert Eagles"[1]

It was just past dawn on 25 July 2005, a day already quite warm and
dusty, when the combat reconnaissance patrol led by CPT Christopher
Wells made contact with the enemy in Syahcow, Afghanistan. The patrol's
lead element, separated from the main body, came under heavy rifle and
machine gun fire from the village. As the lead element attempted to maneuver on the enemy, the patrol then came under heavy and accurate direct
and indirect fire from the mountain slopes to the west. Wells, in the con-
fusing first moments of contact, saw he faced a prepared and determined
enemy who was engaging his force from several different directions and
with significantly more firepower than he had at his disposal.

Later, Wells remembered the first thing he wanted to do was find out
where his separated lead element was and the exact location of the force
he had sent out to establish a blocking position to the southeast of his position. At the same time, the Taliban was bringing in accurate and effective
mortar, machine gun, rocket propelled grenade (RPG), and even recoilless
rifle fire against his outgunned patrol. The initial tenacity of the enemy
confirmed much of the intelligence his Special Forces A Team had developed. Now, the decisions Wells would make along with the actions of his
Soldiers would determine if the Coalition forces and the Afghan National
Army could defeat the Taliban power and influence in the Oruzgan province of Afghanistan.[2]

The 1st Battalion, 3d Special Forces Group, took over sector responsibility of southern Afghanistan in July 2005. Designated Task Force (TF)
31, the battalion was provided with additional resources and had responsibility for special operations activities in southern Afghanistan. The battalion commander, LTC Don Bolduc, and his battalion, known as the Desert
Eagles, knew the area well as this was the unit's third deployment to southern Afghanistan in 3 years.[3]

In the months before taking charge of the sector, the Desert Eagles
conducted a thorough assessment of the region, people, and nature of the

enemy they would face. The enemy, they concluded, had changed significantly since their last deployment. Bolduc felt the insurgency had reconstituted and matured close to the level of open guerrilla warfare. The anticoalition militia (ACM) was recruiting, training, and operating in the sanctuary provinces of Oruzgan, northwest Zabul, and northern Kandahar.[4] To accomplish his assigned missions, Bolduc developed a strategy to defeat the insurgency:

> The way I see our mission in Afghanistan is the conduct of selected unconventional warfare tasks in a counterinsurgency environment as it applies to our areas in southern Afghanistan. During this rotation, my responsibilities were all Special Operations Forces (SOF) in southern Afghanistan and under a specific strategy designed to search for the enemy, find, fix, and finish him, and attack him both kinetically and non-kinetically through the use of direct and indirect approaches. Assist the local populace through the use of civil-military operations (CMO), psychological operations (PSYOP), and information operations (IO), and then train the Afghan National Army (ANA) along a decentralized program of instruction and assist other Afghan national security forces to be able, over time, to do what we're doing and work ourselves out of a job. So that's not a standard mission statement but that's how I understand it and that's how we approached it.[5]

Bolduc built his strategy and focused on the methods of search, attack, assist, and train. He deployed his force throughout his assigned sector in firebases oriented toward challenging the enemy in the sanctuary areas. From these firebases, Operational Detachment Alpha (ODA) or A Teams would implement the strategy. The strategy focused on the population and on the enemy. Toward the people, activities were designed to address their needs, separate them from the insurgents, and develop support for the government of Afghanistan. Toward the enemy, the Desert Eagles would patrol aggressively and challenge the insurgents in the heart of the ACM and Taliban sanctuaries. The method is simply stated as pressure, pursue, and punish. (See map 8.)

The combat patrols Bolduc wanted to conduct against the enemy were built around the ODA. Typically, there are 3 companies of 6 teams or 18 total ODAs in a battalion. The ODA is a 12-man team with a captain as its leader. A warrant officer or a chief warrant officer serves as the team's

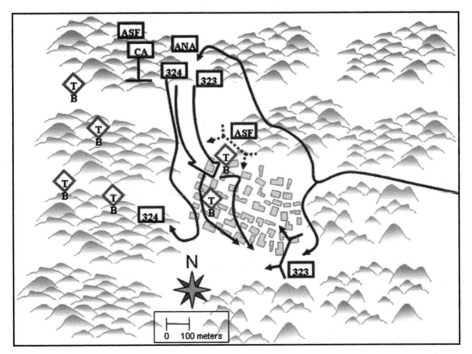

Map 8. Syahcow, Afghanistan, 25 July 2005.

second in command. The operations sergeant or team sergeant is a master sergeant and the intelligence sergeant, who also serves as the assistant operations sergeant, is a sergeant first class. The remainder of the team is comprised of two senior noncommissioned officers (NCOs) per functional area of weapons, engineer, medical, and communications. Team members are cross-trained in different specialties and are multilingual.[6]

The ODAs, mounted in ground mobility vehicles (GMV), conducted the combat patrols with their Afghan allies. The Special Forces GMV, built on the Humvee (HMMWV) chassis, featured improved armor, a turbo-diesel engine, and a turret capable of mounting a .50-caliber machine gun or MK47 automatic grenade launcher. The Afghan army or Afghan security force elements would travel in Toyota pickup trucks.

The working relationship between the Afghan forces and the Special Forces Soldiers at the time was good. The US forces fought with the same units they trained. CPT Paul Toolan, a battalion operations officer, described the unique partnership with the Afghan army in that they welcomed the Afghan army into their operations center, and if there were a large operation, they would station an ANA liaison officer with the US force. To support the development of the ANA as a force capable of conducting the future security mission, Toolan said it was important to provide the ANA with the tools and intelligence they needed to succeed.[7]

The patrols often took the form of a combat reconnaissance patrol. These patrols were flexibly designed for use in conventional missions and in unconventional operations. One important role of the combat reconnaissance patrol was that of conducting harassing operations in areas of extensive guerrilla activity. These patrols were used to determine if an enemy force was present in an area and, if so, maintain contact until the enemy force was destroyed.[8] These patrols contained enough men and firepower to overcome most types of enemy operations such as attacks or ambushes. With the long distances between friendly bases, these patrols would potentially have to fight alone successfully for long periods before supporting firepower or forces could assist them. For example, it could take from 30 to 45 minutes before close air support (CAS) could provide supporting fires or up to 2 hours before a helicopter could bring in a quick reaction force (QRF).

The flexible design and structure of the combat reconnaissance patrol was necessary because of the limited number of supporting US and Coalition forces in southern Afghanistan. Most actionable enemy intelligence was gained by the Soldiers while on patrol or in support missions designed to assist the people. There usually was enough intelligence to plan a patrol or to confirm or deny the information, but rarely enough to justify in advance the expenditure of major resources such as planned aviation fires or the use of conventional forces. Thus, the teams would plan and conduct the patrols with enough of their own combat power to find, fix, and finish the enemy if they found him.

Syahcow (Siah Chow) is a small village of about 25 to 30 typical Afghan compound-type buildings in the Oruzgan province. On trying to locate it, Toolan said, "It's a blip on the map and you generally wouldn't find it because it's not annotated."[9] The Helmand River is to its east and the Siah Ghub and Dizak Ghar Mountains are to its west. Syahcow is 20 kilometers southwest of the district capital, Deh Rawud, and 25 kilometers from Firebase Tycz. The key units stationed at Firebase Tycz were ODA 323 and ODA 324. Wells, responsible for the Deh Rawud district, was in command of the firebase. Syahcow was becoming the center point of the growing enemy strength in the Deh Rawud district. To the west were several trails that served the ACM as infiltration and supply corridors. SFC Don Grambusch of ODA 324 knew the Taliban presence was strong in the mountainous area to the west of Syahcow, and since his arrival, had observed an increase in the enemy propaganda influence south of Firebase Tycz.[10]

The Desert Eagles found the best and most useful source of intelligence to be the people of Afghanistan. What the people told the Soldiers of ODA 324 was that the Taliban were building strength in the Syahcow area and, as of June 2005, had between 150 to 200 fighters in the area. The Taliban would come into a town to gather supplies and recruit—their recruiting method was to demand the young men of the village join their force or they would kill the men's families. The Taliban leader in the Deh Rawud district was Mullah Abdul Wali. Wells learned Abdul Wali had recently kidnapped and beheaded two people from the area.

During the transition period in which the Desert Eagles assumed control of the sector, Abdul Wali had taken the mountain pass to the west of Syahcow and attacked the town of Tagaw. Abdul Wali lost the fight suffering 30 to 40 killed in action to include 2 of his commanders, and he himself was wounded and fled to Pakistan to recover. Interestingly, the Afghan national police withstood his attack and defeated him. In addition, some of the local villagers joined in the fight, helping the police defeat the Taliban.

Relative quiet returned to the sector while Abdul Wali recovered. Then in late July, the local people reported that Abdul Wali had returned and had taken over Syahcow. The intelligence indicated he had returned with about 20 to 30 fighters, driven all the inhabitants away, and brought Syahcow totally under the control of the Taliban. Reports even stated he had raised his flag over the village.[11] Wells and his team believed the intelligence, but to verify it they had to physically check the village:

> Well, we decided to act on Siah Chow getting this intel, realizing he was there with his core fighters and probably hadn't had the time to go around and gather anybody else up. We wanted to go ahead and take care of him and his core fighters. So we quickly task organized and knew there was probably going to be a fight, but we weren't positive. Our mission statement was a reconnaissance patrol to confirm or deny their existence in that town. It wasn't a movement to contact on paper but we planned it that way. We planned for the worst, hoped for the best."[12]

Using the military decisionmaking process (MDMP), the detachment conducted a thorough planning session. The MDMP is a detailed way to plan by developing possible scenarios called courses of action that are then tested by wargaming possible enemy and friendly actions. The result of this process is a plan that has been carefully designed and analyzed, and may include various options in case the operation does not develop the way the plan predicts. Wells and the members of his detachment expected the Taliban to defend the village. They knew the enemy to be hardened fighters who were not likely to give in or scatter, as did lesser forces of the Taliban. The plan's level of detail extended to the establishment of barrier positions to block anyone from entering or departing and then clearing the village compound by compound. Grambusch thought the detailed planning was beneficial, and aware that the first shot always changes the plan and in combat luck always plays a role, he thought the detailed planning "put a better chance of luck, in [our] favor."[13]

Wells decided to bring as much combat power with him as he could. He conscripted his Civil Affairs Team to provide additional external security with their Humvee mounted .50-caliber machine guns. He also packed the detachment's 60-mm mortar, a weapon not always brought on patrol. In addition to his own ODA 324, he took along ODA 323, which was without a team leader and consisted of only five Soldiers. Another important force element in his plan was the Afghan forces. He brought 50 Afghan Security Forces personnel and 30 Afghan army soldiers.[14] If he had to physically clear the village, their additional combat power would be critical to the success of the mission. In addition, the two Special Forces NCOs of the Embedded Training Team (ETT) who were providing training support to the ODAs volunteered to join the patrol.

Last, Wells briefed his company commander and the Desert Eagle Operations Center on the plan. This not only provided situational awareness for his senior commanders, but gave them the opportunity to assist him with additional intelligence and combat resources. The headquarters for TF 31 was located at Kandahar as were most of the command and control (C2) elements and many of the resources for southern Afghanistan. Thus, TF 31 was able to quickly provide a warning order up to Task Force *Storm*, the aviation task force, and the quick reaction force, Company C, 2d Battalion (Airborne), 503d Infantry Regiment, of the impending patrol.

Wells planned to arrive and establish the cordon around the village at sunrise. To arrive at sunrise, the patrol departed Firebase Tycz at 2 a.m. on 25 July 2005. The patrol proceeded to the Helmand River ford sites the ODA had used in previous patrols, crossed, and proceeded north to Syahcow. Though uneventful, two minor victories occurred during the movement—light discipline and the fording of the Helmand River. While US Special Forces teams are trained and equipped to operate at night using night observation devices (NODs), the Afghan soldiers were not equipped with NODs and so had difficulty operating at night. The Afghan soldiers had to be persuaded not to use their headlights in their Toyota pickup trucks. Fortunately, the weather was clear and, with almost a full moon providing illumination, the Afghan vehicles rolled without headlights. The second success came at the ford site. The depth of the water was such that the Toyotas had to back through the water at the ford to keep the engines from dying. According to Grambusch, the fording, while exciting, was completed in about the same amount of time as a daytime operation.[15]

As the patrol came out of the ford site, it returned to its formation and began to move north. Because of the terrain, the patrol was road bound. In the lead was four Special Forces Soldiers mounted on all-terrain vehicles (ATV). Their task was to move ahead of the patrol, ensure the route was clear, and serve as a forward reconnaissance element. Next, in the order of march, were the Afghan Special Forces (ASF) and ANA personnel, and following them were the ODAs mounted in their GMVs. This was a fairly standard formation for combat reconnaissance patrols. The lead element on the ATVs usually included at least one engineer specialist to assess the route, look for improvised explosive devices (IED), or in the case of contact provide early warning. Next, the ASF and ANA element was an infantry maneuver element ready to react to the enemy. If ambushed, the Special Forces Soldiers would move forward to advise and assist the Afghan forces and assess the situation. If necessary, they could also provide heavy weapons support to the Afghan units. The route from the ford took the patrol parallel to and north of Syahcow. Taking this route allowed the patrol to occupy the terrain to the north of the village. It also allowed them to occupy the high ground closest to the village. Even better, a hill mass located just east of Syahcow masked their movement from the village.

The patrol moved into the hills north of Syahcow and began negotiating the trail southward toward the village. The terrain was difficult to negotiate so two ATVs went forward on reconnaissance while two guided the vehicles along the trail. Their luck seemed to be holding until, in Grambusch's words, "The two lead ATVs were a little further ahead and at that point the lead GMV came around the corner, a front wheel went in a wadi and it turned over on its side. This is just as the sun is coming up, we're about 5 minutes of the objective and well within sound of the objective."[16] Wells quickly decided to proceed with the plan. While using another GMV to recover the overturned vehicle, he dispatched two ATVs to lead one GMV from ODA 323 southeast to a hill that isolated and blocked the southern routes out of the village. He intended that hill to be a support by fire position in case of contact. The ATVs then returned to the main body north of the village. The recovery of the flipped GMV was almost complete and the southern blocking position was set.

Wells knew he had little time now to isolate the village. It was nearly 0500, the sun was coming up and the recovery of the flipped vehicle had been so noisy that he feared the patrol's location had been compromised. He had expected only light security at dawn. As he later explained:

> We theorized that the Taliban were going to be pretty tired because we received information that they were taking the bodies of the guys who were killed in Tagaw and bringing them back to Syahcow and burying them. So they had been burying these guys for a day or two and we figured they would be pretty smoked. What's more, they were probably not the most devout of Muslims who would be getting up early in the morning for prayer; and if they did, it would be lip service and they'd go right back to sleep. So we knew their security would be pretty lax at the time.[17]

With the main element almost ready to move, he wanted to observe the village to see if they had disrupted the enemy's activities. If the enemy was leaving, he wanted to put somebody on the northern blocking position. Therefore, he ordered the four ATVs to move to the crest of the northern hills overlooking Syahcow.

Especially important assets to the ODAs in Afghanistan were their ATV sections. Each ODA normally operated with two ATVs, and because there were two ODAs, Wells had four he could employ. If properly employed and skillfully manned, the element provided a flexible tool the commander could use to influence a fluid or challenging situation. Wells knew proper manning was the key to success and had previously decided to put some of his most experienced NCOs in the ATV element. This decision also placed the team's senior engineer specialist in the element, a Soldier expert in identifying and clearing obstacles and who could judge the terrain in a reconnaissance with an experienced eye. He also placed an experienced senior NCO, an assistant operations and intelligence specialist, and two Special Forces medic NCOs on the team.

On Wells' order, the four ATVs moved to the crest of the hill and immediately radioed in "Squirters!" A squirter was the term applied to individuals who tried to get out or run away from the objective area. The team observed two such individuals in local garb running out of town toward a hill to the southwest. In accord with the team's standing operating procedure, three of the ATVs moved off the hill heading in a southwesterly direction to cut off the squirters. The procedural drill, in which the ATVs interdicted people trying to depart the objective area, had been named "bulldogging."[18]

Grambusch, on the fourth ATV, stayed on the crest to serve as the radio relay between the main body, which was beginning to move toward his location, and the three ATVs. The three ATVs had immediately descended the steep hillside and were beginning to work their way through the rough undulating terrain on the west side of the village. The path they were taking would lead them to a small hill on the southwest side of town where they could intercept the two fleeing individuals. Grambusch observed, "As soon as those three ATVs came parallel to the village, the whole western side of the village erupted in a huge volley of gunfire: automatic weapons fire, AK47s and rocket propelled grenades (RPGs)." He immediately reported the contact to Wells, who was just bringing the main body to Grambusch's position on the crest of the hill to establish the northern blocking position.[19] Grambusch saw at least eight rocket propelled grenades impact very near the three ATVs.

The three ATV riders, SFC Larry Hawks, SFC Bruce Holmes, and SFC Bob Thibeault, still mounted, tried to evade the intense and murderous fire. Hawks, the lead ATV, moved up to the high ground directly to his front, a position to the immediate southwest of Syahcow, dismounted his ATV, and immediately started returning fire. Among the rocks of a bald desert hill, from his still exposed position, he killed four of the enemy. For his actions on this day, he was recommended for the Distinguished Service Cross. At the same time, Holmes was trying get out of the kill zone of his closest attackers. Holmes' ATV was hit several times and became stuck in the muddy low ground of a streambed he was trying to move through. He was pinned in the streambed until Hawks' accurate fire allowed him to mount his ATV and move to Hawks' position. Meanwhile, Thibeault maneuvered his ATV away from the direct fire of his assailants and observed several individuals, including the two original squirters, in a position west and uphill of Hawks' new position. Seeing the danger as the enemy began to fire on Hawks, Thibeault moved up and began to engage the enemy, killing two and driving off the rest. He then joined Hawks. Grambusch, from the high ground north of the village, was firing into the village, both to protect the ATV element and his own position. Wells, having received the contact reports, brought the main body up to the crest of the northern hill and established contact with Grambusch.

Wells also learned that his combat reconnaissance patrol was involved in a significant fight. His two elements south of the village, the GMV on the hill to the southeast and the ATV element on the high ground to the southwest, were returning an increasingly high volume of fire coming from the village. Then the nature of the battle changed again when enemy fighters on the mountains to the west of the village began to fire on the three exposed US and Afghan positions with mortars, RPGs, and PKM machine guns. This fire, which ranged from as close as a few hundred meters out to 2 kilometers, was very effective. As Wells observed, "They had obviously fired at these locations before, dialed the ranges, and they had a plan for someone to come upon them that way—because they were able to immediately put fire right on us."[20] As Wells was taking in the situation, a piece of shrapnel hit one of his best weapons, the MK47 grenade launcher, and knocked it out of the fight. Then large caliber rounds began striking his position from a new enemy location in the mountains to the west. His team quickly identified the position as a cave within 900 to 1,000 meters and the weapon as a recoilless rifle, most probably a Soviet made SPG-9.

As Wells surveyed the situation, he found two of his three elements under heavy direct and indirect fire and pinned down. The enemy force was similar in size to his, but had the advantage in accurate firepower and tactical positioning. Wells knew the decisions he would make in the next few hours would significantly affect the battle for southern Afghanistan and the survival of his unit. Furthermore, Wells knew he had limited choices, and as he explains, "Normally if we didn't have an element pinned down in the south, I could have pulled off, called for CAS." He knew that whatever course he chose he would have to support it and relieve the pressure on his elements in contact. He knew it was a matter of 30 to 45 minutes before CAS would be on station. One option was to remain in the northern position, return fire, and wait for the CAS to provide decisive fires. Another option was to maintain the current northern position as a support by fire position and begin maneuvering on and destroying enemy positions to relieve the stress on the element that was pinned down to the southwest. A third feasible option was to attempt to disengage from the north and then move along the previously covered route to the south and link up with the pinned element.

*   *   *

Wells decided to provide fire from his position until CAS was available. The enemy fire from the western mountain slopes was the most dangerous to the three-man ATV element pinned down in the southwest and to his northern element. Once CAS was on station, he knew he could change the battlefield calculus to his advantage. He also knew the most dangerous weapon available to the enemy was the mortar positioned on the western slopes. His force in the north could disperse and find some cover from the SPG-9 recoilless rifle and small arms fire, but the mortar was attacking him with accurate indirect fire. With his MK47 disabled, the 60-mm mortar represented his best weapon to suppress the enemy mortars. Wells ordered its employment and, within a few minutes, the American counter-mortar fire suppressed the enemy mortar position.

On first contact, Wells had reported in to the TF 31 Tactical Operations Center (TOC) and had requested CAS. A few minutes later, when he was able to make a better assessment, he provided a more detailed report to the TOC and the battalion commander. Wells' first thought was to identify the locations of all of his Soldiers. He could see them, but he needed to confirm exact locations before the CAS arrived. He knew the enemy pinned down his elements, but his three positions also isolated the enemy force in Syahcow. His first priority was to maintain those positions, then use them to his advantage by eliminating the fire he was receiving from the mountains to the west.[21]

At the TF 31 TOC, the operations officer, MAJ Richard Reese, and the battle captain, CPT William Hart, began coordinating for the CAS and other needed battalion assets. Bolduc, the battalion commander, discussed the situation with Wells and decided he would ask the commander of Regional Command (RC) South for the QRF. While Toolan coordinated the request, Bolduc spoke with the RC South commander about his assessment and request for the QRF. Then Bolduc informed the Combined Joint Special Operations Task Force (CJSOTF) of the situation.

Approximately 45 minutes later, CAS was on station in the form of a British GR-7, the United Kingdom's version of the Harrier fighter aircraft. The patrol did not have an Air Force Combat Controller so Wells served the function of working the CAS onto target. The GR-7 had a 1,000-pound bomb and Wells and the pilot had agreed on a target when an unknown controller misidentified friendly markings. Wells had stated the nearest friendly troops were marked with red smoke, which was all they had, when suddenly a voice over the radio stated that red smoke marked the enemy. Wells suspected it was an airborne C2 element, but he had to delay the bombing until he sorted things out. The GR-7 was then positioned to support the operation from a safe and distant position as two Apache attack helicopters arrived on station. Quickly, one of the Apache pilots was able to get the exact coordinates of the SPG-9 position by using his laser range finder. That gave the GR-7 the opportunity to provide the air support still needed by the patrol. The GR-7 bombed the SPG-9 position with a single bomb. The Apache pilots also provided fires on the western mountain positions. The fires provided by the CAS and the patrols' own 60-mm mortar changed the battle in favor of the Coalition forces. The western ridgeline was now devoid of enemy activity. Those not killed had departed the battle area or had retreated to caves in the mountains.

The three Coalition positions now represented a cordon to prevent any enemy in the village from escaping. Wells positioned the Apaches to help kill or capture enemy fighters in the village. Anticipating they might have to clear the village, the Special Forces officers and NCOs along with their Afghan allies had wargamed the clearing plan and took measures to communicate and coordinate with everybody in the patrol. The first measure was to have everyone operate on the same radio frequency and manage one network of friendly call signs. They believed this simple procedure would enhance both communication and flexibility by each person hearing, in real time, the reports of the other team members. The second tool they employed was a battleship matrix. The battleship matrix was a grid template overlaid on a satellite photograph of the Syahcow area. The grid reference system provided a quick orientation tool. Additionally, to enhance coordination and awareness, they numbered each of the compounds.[22]

Less than 2 hours after the first shots were fired, Wells ordered the clearing teams to move forward. His northern position was secure with the firepower of the GMVs and the ASF security element. MSG Keith Logsdon, the team sergeant for ODA 324, led the two clearing teams from the northern position taking a route from the northeast downward to the southwest to the first compound. They came under fire from the village as they moved downhill toward the first compound. The route that offered the best cover to approach the first compound was a dry creek bed. The team entered the creek bed and continued moving to the compound at the same time as three enemy fighters were attempting to reposition in the same creek bed. Logsdon observed the three Taliban fighters and immediately killed them.[23]

Once they cleared the first compound, Logsdon was supposed to take one team to the west side of town and clear from north to south. The other team, on the east side and also clearing from north to south, was led by SFC Willie Bell of ODA 323. The concept was for the teams to alternate clearing compounds, maintaining alignment, and remaining within supporting range of each other. Each team was supposed to consist of one squad of the ANA led by a Special Forces NCO. However, as the day wore on, the intense heat and combat took its toll. Personnel from different elements of the patrol rotated in and out of these teams. Additionally, personnel from the ASF volunteered and rotated in to relieve the soldiers from the ANA. Late in the day, Logsdon was in danger of becoming a heat casualty so Thibeault relieved him. Also, the two members of the ETT and Soldiers from the US Civil Affairs unit accompanied the clearing teams.

Wells faced another hard question as the teams fought their way into the first compounds. Specifically, were there still civilians in the village? Early in the fight the GMV stationed on the hill to the southeast observed a woman and child move through and out of the battle area. With his assault teams fighting their way to the village, he had to decide whether to use the Apaches in the very close support role he needed as his teams cleared the objective. As he later explained:

> After the gunfight started and we started trying to move into the village, every compound we tried to clear we received fire from, so it made it very easy to make the decision to go ahead and engage it with whatever I had available. I was not going to put my guys into a compound that they were receiving a lot of fire from if I didn't have to before I hit it with rockets and machine guns from the Apaches. That was the main thing. Once we realized, 'Hey, there's no one here,' all right, we're not holding back anything; we're just going to go ahead and do what we need to do to get through the town. A lot of people above us couldn't believe there wasn't anybody in the town, but that's what our intel had said, which we confirmed; everybody we took out of the town was taken with a weapon or a weapon was taken off their body. We were 100 percent positive that there wasn't anyone else in the town except for the combatants. You could see they were prepared to fight; they took their turbans off and tied them around their waists. Upon talking with one of my interpreters, they have a saying like our, 'Pull up your boot straps' when you're getting ready to work. Well, they say, 'Tie your turban around your waist' when they're getting ready to do some hard work. That was a clear signal—that all of them were dressed like that—that they knew they were there to fight the whole day.[24]

Wells brought in the Apaches and coordinated their fires on the different compounds in the village. However, the small clearing force was too small to take on the number of Taliban in the village. Logsdon held up the entire clearing force in the wadi on the northeast side of town and directed the Apaches to soften up the target area. Then, at 0800 the QRF reached the landing zone just north of the northern blocking position. A rifle platoon from Company C, 2d Battalion (Airborne) of the 503d Infantry Regiment, 173d Airborne Brigade disembarked from two CH-47 helicopters. Once the platoon was on the ground, Wells wanted to get them into the fight. "They landed, I gave the team leader one of my battleship matrices of the town, briefed them on what was going on, told them this was not a typical QRF and that they were here to fight today. I said, there are Taliban in the town and we're fighting them right now. I made it very clear to them they were going to fight some bad guys today."[25] Wells then, in coordination with the QRF platoon leader, divided the QRF into two sections and assigned each to one of the two clearing teams. The QRF teams moved down to the wadi outside the village and joined their respective teams. Logsdon took charge of them, then he and Bell started clearing Syahcow.

Bolduc, at the Desert Eagle (TF 31) TOC, was satisfied that the tactical situation was now in hand. He next thought to identify assets he could use for a multitiered effect on the enemy and on the population in the Helmand River Valley. He wanted to pile on, he wanted to get the enemy commander, he wanted Syahcow to be a statement. Additionally, intelligence was feeding him information that specific high value targets were in the next couple of villages and towns. He spoke with MAJ Chris Hensley, the B Company Commander, who was at Tarin Kowt, and ordered him to go to Syahcow and take over control of the fight. He also wanted Hensley to bring more force multipliers to the battle, an additional ODA Team, more medics, and better C2 assets. Later, when Hensley arrived, Bolduc would push additional assets to him. Then Bolduc and Hensley would plan a shaping operation that would last several more days.

Up to this point, Grambusch, running the patrol's casualty collection point (CCP), the main medical aid station, had to deal with one serious casualty. The casualty was a soldier from the ANA. The CCP was in the same vicinity as the QRF helicopter-landing zone. He first initiated what would become the norm for medical evacuations (MEDEVAC) throughout the battle. He described it as a nonstandard MEDEVAC. He loaded the wounded Afghan soldier on board one of the CH-47s and had them transport the wounded soldier to the closest medical treatment facility. It was nonstandard because the helicopter was not equipped for MEDEVAC operations as it had no life-saving resources, interpreters, or trained medical personnel. Grambusch had to talk the crew into transporting the wounded Afghan over their initial concerns about not being able to care for the soldier.

Wells wanted to reinforce the southern blocking position as the clearing teams moved from north to south. At this point, if the enemy disengaged, they would try to move in a southerly direction, and he wanted to have a sufficient mobile force available to deal with any contingencies. Wells also wanted to be in a better position to control his forces and the southern position offered better observation of the battlefield. Just prior to the arrival of the QRF, Wells handed off the control of the Apaches to Hawks at the southwestern ATV position. At this point, Hawks had better observation of the enemy positions, the compounds in Syahcow, and he was very experienced at controlling aircraft in a ground support mission. Thus, Wells decided to move to the blocking position held by the ATV element. He would take with him the C2 systems and the bulk of the forces holding the northern blocking position. Grambusch would also move the CCP south with Wells. Wells left a strong blocking force in the north, then moved south, around the village, until he joined the ATV element. It proved fortuitous for the men in the ATV element, as they were running very short on water and ammunition.

The two clearing teams, reinforced by the paratroopers of the 503d Airborne Infantry, began clearing the village, compound by compound. Initially each team consisted of the Special Forces NCO in charge, an ANA squad, and the section of the US Infantry platoon. If the compound was active and the clearing team was receiving fire, then the team directed AH-64 Apache helicopters to engage the compound. The team leader, initially Logsdon or Bell, would direct the ANA squad to assault and secure the compound; once secure, the US Infantry force would conduct a detailed search. Wells had everyone operating on one radio network and frequency. This allowed Logsdon and Bell to coordinate their movements and provide support for the teams as they leapfrogged from compound to compound. It also provided all members of the patrol with the latest information on where each team was located. Once a team had secured a compound and was supporting the move of the other team or ready to assault the next compound, they painted the number of the compound on the outer wall using spray paint. This mark indicated to all that a team had been in the compound. The number was the same one designated on the battleship matrix used to coordinate the battle.

Clearing a building or a series of buildings is extremely dangerous, hard to coordinate, very hard to keep coordinated, and stressful and exhausting to the Soldiers. Typically, in training environments, it eats up units and Soldiers. Syahcow, on this very hot day in July proved no different. Wells continued,

We were fighting in 115-degree temperatures, everybody was getting smoked really quickly, but we still had to continue to fight and clear through the village. Well, about halfway through the village, the ANA, to my surprise—because they're usually the guys who can run up a mountain on a quarter jug of water and not breathe hard at all while we're stuck at the bottom, still trying to make our way up—the heat just started getting to them and some of them couldn't continue on fully. We had to start giving them rest breaks in the middle of the fight, which I thought was pretty unusual. They were so tired that they just did not want to go on.[26]

The ASF, who were supposed to provide only security, started to volunteer to replace the Afghan Army soldiers as they went down from heat and exhaustion. Additionally, the Special Forces teams had the ETT who had accompanied them on the patrol and who had gone in with the clearing teams. Even the Civil Affairs team had joined the close quarters fight. The robust manning of the teams proved beneficial as the heat took its toll even on the most experienced US Soldiers. Later in the day, even Logsdon was overcome by the heat and had to be relieved by Thibeault.

Clearing the village did not come without cost. In the end, the Coalition force suffered two killed in action, one US NCO from the 2d Battalion (Airborne), 503d Infantry QRF, and one Afghan from the ASF. Additionally, there were five wounded: two US and three Afghans. At the cost of SSG Michael Schafer's life, the clearing teams learned the key to the enemy's defense. This knowledge prevented them from considering the village secure until the next day. The key tactic the enemy was using to successfully engage the Coalition forces and protect themselves from the devastating attacks of the Apache helicopters was the village's fresh water supply system. Schafer, while conducting a detailed search, was shot from the village's underground aqueduct system. The system carried water from the mountains to the village and was interconnected throughout the village. To the clearing teams, the aqueduct system appeared as large holes in the ground. These deep craters connected the channels and were large enough for the Taliban fighters to move through. This allowed the fighters to survive the overwhelming attacks of the Apaches and maneuver to the previously cleared compounds in the rear to continue the fight. The clearing teams lacked the combat power to clear the village and the aqueduct system; therefore, they did not send anyone down into the aqueduct system. They did use grenades, rifles, and automatic weapons to clear each aqueduct hole as they continued to clear each compound. The teams, understanding and mitigating the threat, did not lose anyone else to the aqueduct system.

The other fatality was an ASF squad leader. A GMV and ASF security element from ODA 323 had pushed forward to the northwest edge of the village to provide cover for the clearing teams. The squad leader, at the front of the element, was wounded by enemy rifle fire; he rose to signal he was okay and was then shot through the head. While the element returned fire, a second MK47 automatic grenade launcher was disabled and the US Special Forces gunner severely wounded in the hand and arm. The return fire from the remainder of the element killed the sniper. One other US Soldier from the QRF was shot through both legs while part of a clearing team. All wounded US and Afghan Coalition partners were brought to the CCP and treated by the Special Forces medics. The wounded were evacuated to the CCP by the most expeditious means available, often a GMV. One severely wounded Afghan soldier was even evacuated by Bell who carried him in an underarm fashion through intense fire. Those whose wounds were serious enough were evacuated by helicopter. These MEDEVAC flights were from a landing zone established near the southwest blocking position, but covered from direct fire by the hill mass. They were all, technically, nonstandard evacuations, as the helicopters used were the same ones that brought in the QRF and later arriving forces. Again, these helicopters did not have any trained medical personnel to treat the wounded, and did not offer a translator or emergency medical supplies.[27]

Operationally, the tactical situation at Syahcow offered Bolduc an opportunity to pressure and pursue the enemy. He realized he could enhance the disruption Wells' patrol had caused the enemy if he was able to identify enemy targets, bring enough resources to bear, and continue to press the enemy. With the intelligence feed identifying possible enemy targets in Dizak, about 7 kilometers northeast of Syahcow, an opportunity appeared to present itself. He had already ordered Hensley to the battlefield to take charge. Along with the Bravo Company commander, the necessary C2 systems and an additional ODA were moving to the fight. Now it was up to Bolduc to brief the RC South commander to obtain additional resources, specifically, more conventional units to continue the fight.

Hensley arrived as afternoon turned to evening, and Wells' clearing teams were in the final stages of clearing the last compounds. Hensley received an update from Wells and took command. In practice, this meant that Hensley provided the information and reporting structure to battalion headquarters while Wells concentrated on finishing the current fight. Hensley concentrated on oversight of the engaged force and reception of the additional resources Bolduc was pushing to him. About an hour after he arrived, he began future operational planning.[28]

Wells immediately made use of the additional medical support Hensley had brought by pushing the medics forward and into the fight. He held the third ODA in reserve. Bolduc also sent an additional Infantry QRF of platoon size and a 105-mm artillery battery of four howitzers. The immediate intent of the artillery was to protect the force if it was again engaged from the mountains and ridgelines to the west. Wells also held the follow-on QRF in reserve. There were, as darkness fell over Syahcow, 249 Coalition soldiers on the ground. Once the last compound was clear of enemy forces, Wells and Hensley pulled all friendly troops out of the village while still maintaining the cordon around it.[29]

Wells, throughout the fight in the village, had not forgotten the enemy that had engaged him from the mountains and ridgelines to the west, and who had most probably gotten away. Even during the more tense moments of the battle, he had longed for the resources in men, mobility, and firepower to have gone after that enemy. As the day was ending, he led a patrol to one of the positions in the western mountains from which his force had been engaged. It proved to be larger than anticipated. Inside a cave they found an 82-mm mortar, a machine gun, and a mix of ammunition, all of which they destroyed. The cave was very narrow and deep, and they did not have the time to clear it properly so they were unable to determine what trails the Taliban were using.

Night brought an end to the fight for Syahcow. The Soldiers of the Desert Eagles, the 2d Battalion (Airborne), 503d Infantry, and their Afghan partners had punished the enemy, and Hensley and Wells were planning to punish the enemy again the next day. The action had been a heroic small unit fight, instructive at several levels. The NCOs and Soldiers acted competently, professionally, and heroically throughout the course of the day in accomplishing their mission. Examples of these Soldiers heroically doing their duty include the stout defense of the exposed southwestern blocking position by the ATV element; the brave assault; the clearing of up to 30 different compounds by the Special Forces and Infantry Soldiers; the many medical evacuations in which Soldiers took extreme risk to move their wounded comrades to the rear; the direction of Apache fires well within minimum safe distances to pressure and punish the enemy; and the audacity and valor of the crews of the Apaches who provided the close and accurate fires that ensured the survival and success of the ground units and the mission. They set a standard for duty and valor on this day. Similarly, the Afghan forces proved good allies and partners in the fight. The ASF were at a higher state of readiness than the ANA, but were hamstrung by the rules governing their use. Both the ANA and the ASF proved courageous and developed their skills in urban operations and small unit tactics. They were tested in one of the most challenging combat situations and, working well with their trainers, mentors, and friends validated the training and employment practices followed by the Desert Eagles.

The Coalition force inflicted a defeat on the Taliban. The purpose of the combat reconnaissance patrol was to determine if the enemy was in force and in Syahcow. They had been told a local enemy commander, Abdul Wali, was in Syahcow. The two forces met and the enemy paid dearly for their defensive stand in the village. Even more importantly, the Coalition forces had driven into the sanctuary area where the Taliban thought they were secure, fought them, and disrupted their organization. The price the Taliban paid included 15 confirmed killed and 15 fighters captured. In the defensive belt of the western mountains, they lost an estimated 25 to 30 more fighters and suffered the destruction of a SPG-9 recoilless rifle and an 82-mm mortar along with many smaller caliber weapons and much ammunition.[30] The fight at Syahcow was instructive, as a microcosm of the nature of conflict in Afghanistan, throughout the spectrum of conflict. The Syahcow experience added to the body of knowledge by giving tactical lessons with operational trends and outcomes.

Active ground patrolling proved its worth to all levels of the US-led Coalition. As he took over sector responsibility, Bolduc had concluded that the Taliban influence was growing in the sanctuary areas within southern Afghanistan. The fight at Syahcow proved the Taliban were there, in force, competent, and willing to stand and fight.[31] The Syahcow fight also illustrated the risk involved with active patrolling at both tactical and operational levels. Combat reconnaissance patrols represented an essential piece of the Desert Eagle strategy in southern Afghanistan. It was the best way to pressure, pursue, and punish the enemy. Since Bolduc required the teams to develop their own intelligence that generated each patrol, he expected the patrols would be fighting. To be ready for this contingency, at task force level he established his own QRF. Bolduc also knew if he tried to coordinate these programmed combat operations with RC South, they would compete with every other priority. With resources scarce, he might never get a patrol out the gate. Further, he did not want to commit the scarce resources of RC South on missions where it was equally possible the enemy, if present, would choose not to fight. His guidance to his teams was to plan for the worst, meaning full-scale combat. The risk then became, if a high intensity fight developed, what damage and casualties would the force sustain prior to the 30 to 120 minutes it could take to get emergency CAS on station. The risk was the same if they called for the QRF.

At the tactical and operational levels, how the enemy fought proved very instructive. The enemy was prepared for the battle of Syahcow and was resolute in his defense of the village. Last, the Taliban fighters showed great versatility in shifting their defense as the day wore on. The enemy, during their preparation, identified the aqueduct system as key to their defense, and it proved the key to the survivability of their leadership. After the fight, the team learned Abdul Wali had been in Syahcow and was wounded but had escaped through the aqueduct system. If the enemy center of gravity was their leadership and if leaders such as Abdul Wali were in Syahcow and escaped, then the enemy had identified a dimension of the battlespace the Coalition did not dominate and used it to protect their center of gravity. Even with this advantage, the enemy lost the core of its most reliable fighters in the district and placed Abdul Wali in a position of disadvantage as this operation and others continued to push him, breaking much of his power. Several months later Abdul Wali was killed in another battle. Other aspects of tactical success with operational impact confirmed in this fight were air-ground coordination, team level intelligence, and the cooperation between the US and Afghan forces.

Though the first and only CAS fighter-bomber on station did raise some coordination issues, the pilot and Wells were able to engage the enemy effectively. The team's cooperation with Army aviation was exceptional. This cooperation in most operations is so effective and seamless it is now almost an operational given. The courage and cooperation of both the pilots and the ground forces, however, was so well done it warrants comment. Once the Apaches arrived on station, the battle changed. The enemy, isolated, had to go on the defensive. The Apaches provided extremely accurate and devastating fire throughout the battle. They did this by courageously exposing themselves to defensive fire by sacrificing speed and elevation to ensure accuracy because they knew they were firing dangerously close on most missions. Two Apaches remained on station for over 12 hours of the fight. As one team of two would depart for fuel and ammunition, another team of two would arrive and assume responsibility for the mission.

The idea to conduct a combat reconnaissance patrol was based on solid intelligence developed at the team level and passed upward to higher headquarters. The team members had spoken with many people, some claiming to be from the target village. The message eventually became specific: The

Taliban were in Syahcow and had removed all the people from the village. The Taliban threatened the people and told them not to return. The Taliban raised their flag. This intelligence was the key reason Wells decided to lead the patrol. In this and all other insurgencies, the most useful intelligence was that developed by the units on the ground.

A final note is that of the cooperation between the US and Afghan forces. Since their first rotation in 2002, the Desert Eagles had been working with and building Afghan army and police organizations. In their 2005 rotation, they picked up where they had left off and worked with their counterparts in a cooperative and fully professional manner. They included the ANA and ASF, within limitations, in their planning, pre-execution checks, and team rehearsals. The ANA was usually planned as the main effort, working with the NCOs of the US Special Forces at their side, assisting and advising them. An important combat multiplier in the cooperation between the US forces and the Afghans were the interpreters. Wells' interpreter, Mr. Dost Mohammad, was critical to mission success. Mohammad courageously served throughout the battle, and in his role, he effected critical coordination between the Afghan and US forces. The planning, training, cooperation, and mutual respect paid dividends in the battle of Syahcow where the ANA, the main effort, executed its difficult mission competently and professionally.

The battle of Syahcow represents an example of a tactical operation that had an operational impact and supported the strategy of the 1st Battalion, 3d Special Forces Group commander in southern Afghanistan. It illustrates how organizations and systems operated well together, whether it was the solid relationship of the Coalition partners and Afghan army, or the conventional QRF provided by the 2d Battalion (Airborne), 503d Infantry, or the Apache helicopter crews and the Soldiers on the ground. This successful operation was the first shot at destroying one Taliban cell in the very heart of the Taliban sanctuary. As Wells commented on the leader of that cell, Abdul Wali, "He was the biggest troublemaker in that region and now he's gone."[32]

A year later, on the anniversary of the battle, the members of the Special Forces team met to remember the battle and the sacrifice of SSG Michael Schafer. As Wells put it: "My former teammates and I all met on the 1-year anniversary of the battle of Syahcow in order to remember that without Mike and his fellow infantrymen we might not have survived that day. We will always be in his debt and we will never forget."[33]

Notes

1. LTC Don Bolduc, Commander, TF 31, Fort Bragg, NC, interview by the Operational Leadership Experiences (OLE) Project Team, Combat Studies Institute, digital recording, 26 July 2006, Fort Leavenworth, KS. [Digital recording stored on CD-ROM at Combined Arms Research Library, Fort Leavenworth, KS.]

2. MAJ Christopher B. Wells, Assistant S3, 1-3 SFG, Fort Bragg, NC, interview by the Operational Leadership Experiences (OLE) Project Team, Combat Studies Institute, digital recording, 24 July 2006, Fort Leavenworth, KS. [Digital recording stored on CD-ROM at Combined Arms Research Library, Fort Leavenworth, KS.]

3. "Lying in Wait: Special Operators Say the Taliban is Poised to Wake, Rejuvenated, from a Calculated Slumber," *Army Times*, 16 February 2006, 14–19.

4. Ibid., 17.

5. Bolduc interview.

6. Various sources, Special Forces "A" Team Organizational Structure Fact Sheet, US Army Special Operations Command website, online at <http://www.soc.mil/sf/Ateamfs1.stml>, accessed 19 October 2006.

7. CPT Paul J. Toolan, Commander, HHC 1-3 SFG, Fort Bragg, NC, interview by the Operational Leadership Experiences (OLE) Project Team, Combat Studies Institute, digital recording, 24 July 2006, Fort Leavenworth, KS. [Digital recording stored on CD-ROM at Combined Arms Research Library, Fort Leavenworth, KS.]

8. Various sources, *Tactics, Techniques and Procedures for the Southern Afghanistan Counterinsurgency Fight: PRESSURE, PURSUE, PUNISH*, Fort Bragg, NC, December 2005, 22.

9. Toolan interview.

10. SFC Donald Grambusch, ODA 324, 1-3 SFG, Fort Bragg, NC, interview by the Operational Leadership Experiences (OLE) Project Team, Combat Studies Institute, digital recording, 25 July 2006, Fort Leavenworth, KS. [Digital recording stored on CD-ROM at Combined Arms Research Library, Fort Leavenworth, KS.]

11. Wells interview.

12. Ibid.

13. Grambusch interview.

14. Toolan interview. The ASF was among the first Afghan units trained by SF detachments. The ASF were trained at the firebases and preceded the ANA. They were retained as a security force at the firebases, with their role decreasing in scope as the ANA was established. It ultimately became illegal to conduct offensive operations with the ASF.

15. Grambusch interview.

16. Ibid.

17. Wells interview.

18. Grambusch interview.

19. Ibid.

20. Wells interview.

21. Ibid.

22. Grambusch interview.

23. MAJ Chris Wells briefing, Vignette Brief for the Battle of Syahcow, Deh Rawud, Afghanistan, ODAs 324 and 323, 1st Bn, 3d SFG, 25 July 2005.

24. Wells interview.

25. Ibid.

26. Ibid.

27. Grambusch interview.

28. MAJ Chris Hensley and MAJ Chris Wells, S3, 1-3 SFG, Fort Bragg, NC, interview by the Operational Leadership Experiences (OLE) Project Team, Combat Studies Institute, digital recording, 25 July 2006, Fort Leavenworth, KS. [Digital recording stored on CD-ROM at Combined Arms Research Library, Fort Leavenworth, KS.]

29. Wells briefing.

30. Ibid.

31. LTC Don Bolduc, *Executive Summary of Unconventional Warfare (UW) Assessment, JSOA Carolina and Georgia,* Kandahar, Afghanistan, 16 July 2005, 1–9.

32. Wells interview.

33. MAJ Christopher Wells, e-mail to author, 28 October 2006.

Brave Rifles at Tall 'Afar, September 2005

by

Ricardo A. Herrera

In March 2005, the 3d Armored Cavalry Regiment (ACR), the Brave Rifles of Mexican War fame, deployed from Fort Carson, Colorado, to Kuwait in preparation for operations in northern Babil province, south of Baghdad, Iraq. Commanded by COL H.R. McMaster, it marked the regiment's return to Iraq after previous service in Anbar province during Operation IRAQI FREEDOM (OIF)-I, from April 2003 through May 2004. For the regiment's second rotation, its mission was to conduct counterinsurgency and stability operations in the southern sector of the capital city, including securing Main Supply Route (MSR) TAMPA, Highway 1, running south to north from Kuwait through the Korada and Dŏra districts to Baghdad International Airport, through Mosul, and on to the Turkish border. Leaving Kuwait in early April, the regiment began occupying its new positions in Iraq. For most of the Mounted Riflemen, the stay south of Baghdad was a short one.[1]

Just as the regiment's 2d Squadron "unloaded its last containers in Muhmadiya," Iraq, it assumed a new mission as the lead element in the Brave Rifles' relocation to western Nineveh province, in northwestern Iraq. LTC Christopher M. Hickey, commanding the squadron, received new and "unexpected" orders to conduct counterinsurgent and area security operations in Tall 'Afar and to prepare the area for the reception of the 1st, 4th, and Support Squadrons. Hickey was to have responsibility for Tall 'Afar and its immediate environs, while 1st Squadron operated to the west along the Syrian border, and 4th Squadron flew missions throughout the regimental area of operations (AO).[2]

The Brave Rifles, the Army's sole armored cavalry regiment, brought a powerful mix of ground and aviation assets to the battlefield. Each of its three ground squadrons, organized in three cavalry troops, a tank company, a howitzer battery, and a headquarters troop, fielded 41 M1A2 Abrams Main Battle Tanks, 41 M3A2 Bradley Cavalry Fighting Vehicles, 6 M1064A3 Self-Propelled 120-mm Mortars, and 6 M109A6 Paladin 155-mm Self-Propelled Howitzers. Three air reconnaissance troops totaling 24 Kiowa OH58Ds, two attack troops mustering 16 AH64D Apache Longbows, an assault troop of 15 UH60 Blackhawks, and headquarters and maintenance troops comprised the aviation squadron. Other organic assets included a support squadron, an air defense artillery (ADA) battery with 8 M3 Bradley Stinger Fighting Vehicles and 8 M1097 Avenger Air Defense Systems, the 43d Combat Engineer Company, the 571st Medical Company (Air Ambulance) with 15 UH60s, the 89th Chemical Company, and the 66th Military Intelligence Company. The regiment deployed with its full complement of armored and tracked vehicles.[3]

Originally posted to the "Triangle of Death," with its points at Yusufiyah, Muhmadiyah, and Latifiyah, 2d Squadron was to have relieved 2d Battalion, 70th Armor, part of the 1st Armored Division's 3d Brigade Combat Team (BCT). The AO is agricultural, laced with an extensive canal network that restricts the maneuverability of tracked vehicles. To accomplish its mission, the squadron was to have relied on M1114s. The new mission, however, required that 2d Squadron transfer its two dozen or so high-mobiity multipurpose wheeled vehicles (HMMWVs) to 3d Squadron, under LTC Ross A. Brown, as it assumed responsibility for 2d Squadron's former AO. The 3d Squadron, reinforced by the regiment's air defense battery, a platoon from the 43d Combat Engineer Company, R Troop (Attack Aviation), and 3d Platoon, Company D, 1st Squadron, remained in the Baghdad area, serving at one time or another under two divisional and four brigade-level headquarters.[4]

Tall 'Afar, the new AO for 2d Squadron, was a "hilly agricultural city" of about 150,000 to 200,000 people in northwestern Nineveh, measuring about 9 square kilometers. It lay just over 60 miles east of the Syrian border, about 50 miles west of Mosul, and some 260 miles north of Baghdad. The terrain ranged from open desert and tribal villages to dense urban environments, deep wadis, and even forests. To a very large degree, terrain dictated the regiment's tactics, techniques, and procedures (TTP). In the desert, insurgent attacks at ranges up to 2,000 meters allowed M3A2s, M1A2s, and aviation assets to exploit their long-range optics and the reach of their weapons. Within Tall 'Afar, the city's fabric was as varied as its population. Areas like Hai al-Wahda on the city's west-central side were, by Western standards, a confused arrangement of multistoried buildings, garages, and small alleys.[5]

In spite of the layout, the Mounted Riflemen found areas like the Wahda district "moderately conducive to mounted" operations executed in conjunction with dismounted Soldiers. But Tall 'Afar's east side was an altogether different matter. Places like the older Hai al-Sarai district, which was about 400 by 800 meters in size, had been occupied for over a millennia, and were chock full of "every possible obstacle from modern multistory buildings to ancient houses, caves and even subterranean catacombs." With their narrow alleys and tall buildings, operations in neighborhoods like Sarai limited the maneuverability of armored vehicles. No matter the neighborhood, each mission was a mix of dismounted and mounted elements with tanks, Bradleys, and aviation providing overwatch. Overlooking the city was an Ottoman-era castle, built atop the ruins of previous fortresses dating to the Assyrian empire. The people of Tall 'Afar considered it a symbol of authority.[6]

Tall 'Afar's ethnic and sectarian mix, while not precisely mirroring that of Iraq, was indicative of the ethnic and confessional diversity characterizing the country. It is 90 percent Turkmen, three-quarters of whom are Sunni, the other fourth Shiite, with the remainder of the population Arab, Kurd, and Yezedi. A large number of retired and former noncommissioned officers and specialists with valuable military skills lived in the city. The city lay within a "multi-ethnic belt" bordering Kurdistan, an area rife with tension, in part, because of Sunni Arab fears of "reverse-Arabisation" proposals made by nationalist Kurds hoping to ethnically cleanse the province. It is important to note that Tall 'Afar straddled routes that allowed easy access to Syria and sources of international support.[7]

In 2004 Sunni extremists, known as *Takfiri*, and disenfranchised Iraqi nationalists had come together in a marriage of convenience to seize control of the city and use it as a base of operations for their resistance against American forces and the nascent Iraqi government. For both symbolic and logistical reasons, the city was at the center of Jordanian terrorist Abu Musab al-Zarqawi's strategy of fomenting sectarian violence to undermine the American effort in Iraq. According to the deputy provincial governor of Nineveh, Khasro Goran, over 500 insurgents terrorized the city of nearly a quarter of a million inhabitants through their tactics, which were able to "project a level of fear and intimidation . . . far in excess of the numbers." Tall 'Afar's civic leadership, the little that existed, was suspected of being in league with the insurgents; the over 80 tribes in the region exercised the real leadership. *New York Times* reporter Richard A. Oppel, Jr., called Tall 'Afar a "Magnet for Iraq Insurgents," who had spread their web of influence by taking over distant villages that could provide sanctuary only a "short distance from Mosul . . ., [itself] an active insurgent hub." Insurgents easily passed through holes in the berm demarcating Syria from Iraq and holed up in safe havens scattered about the countryside. Tall 'Afar was a "town that was, for all practical purposes, dead, strangled by the violent insurgents who held it in their thrall."[8]

The intimidation campaign ranged from bombings, assassinations, and mortar and rocket attacks, to beheadings intended to terrify the city's Shiites. In one instance, the insurgents had kidnapped and pressed into service a 14-year old boy. According to Glasgow *Sunday Herald* writer David Pratt, the boy revealed that insurgents had sodomized and "abused" him, and then had assigned him the task of restraining the "legs of victims they beheaded." Hickey recounted that the boy's aim in life was to rise eventually to the point where he would become the executioner. An unnamed Coalition spokesman in Baghdad compared Tall 'Afar to something "'from Mad Max Beyond Thunderdome.'" The insurgents' campaign, despite its viciousness, was neither mindless nor without purpose, although the disparate aims of the constituent groups reflected their equally disparate origins and interests. Insurgent leaders fully appreciated the symbolism in their terrorizing a city that only a year before had been a battlefield for US and Iraqi forces in Operation BLACK TYPHOON.[9]

In 2003 Tall 'Afar had been under the control of the 101st Airborne Division, commanded by MG David Petraeus; by the summer of 2004 a single infantry company from a follow-on unit patrolled the city. According to neurologist Dr. Hakki M. Majdal, deputy director of Tall 'Afar General Hospital, the city's grave economic conditions and growing aggravation over the US occupation of Iraq made the city fertile ground for the insurgency. Led by the Stryker–mounted 3d BCT, 2d Infantry Division, US and Iraqi forces retook the city in fighting that lasted from 9 through 12 September 2004, displacing an estimated 150,000 people, and pushing "reconstruction . . . back to square one." Hoping to resuscitate the city's reconstruction following BLACK TYPHOON, BG Carter F. Ham, commander of Task Force *Olympia*, requested $3 million in emergency funding to rebuild Tall 'Afar's infrastructure, expressing his belief to Mayor Mohammed Rashid Hamid that Tall 'Afar would "'once again be a great city.'" Ham believed, for good reason, that "'Having us stay there [in great strength] is exactly the wrong thing.'" Citing the few American forces available for reoccupying the city, Ham believed that a prolonged American presence conveyed to undecided Iraqis an image of the US as an occupying power. Moreover, Ann Scott Tyson of the *Washington Post*, citing American officers, reported that the poorly disciplined Wolf Brigade, a Shiite police commando outfit, "shot up the [largely Sunni] city," an act the Sunnis perceived as an assault on them.[10]

Ham's estimate of forces and of a prolonged or substantial American presence was correct, but the timing proved precipitate. Indeed, it was part of the larger phenomenon of seizure, clearance, and rapid handover to smaller American forces or to undertrained or ill-prepared Iraqi forces, part of a "cycle that has been repeated in rebellious cities throughout Iraq." According to MAJ Christopher Kennedy, the 3d ACR's executive officer, the impermanence of the American presence and the resulting instability were "'what our lack of combat power has done to us throughout the country. . . . The problem has been we haven't been able to leave sufficient forces in towns where we've cleared the insurgents out.'"[11]

BLACK TYPHOON's success notwithstanding, within a month insurgents reclaimed Tall 'Afar in even greater strength than before. They besieged police stations, severely damaging or destroying some with bombs, forcing terrified residents out of the city, even to the point of the people clearing out of the Sarai neighborhood. The resurgent insurgents' attacks began shortly after dawn prayers on 14 November 2004, the beginning of the *Id al-Fitr* celebration marking the conclusion of Ramadan. They launched a raid on a city prison, freeing the prisoners before bombing it. Continuing their assault, insurgents attacked the police station in the Hassan Qoi district. Interestingly, the sustained assaults started shortly after Operation PHANTOM FURY began on 8 November. At nearly the same time that US and Iraqi forces began the "pacification of Fallujah," Tall 'Afar was replacing Fallujah as a center of the insurgency. Instead of reversing Tall 'Afar's "slide into bedlam," BLACK TYPHOON may have inadvertently hastened it.[12]

As Tall 'Afar slid back into chaos, the insurgents targeted Iraqi security forces and other symbols of government authority. Their attacks thoroughly cowed a police force, once hundreds strong. Through their repeated attacks on stations, the insurgents confined the remaining police to the Ottoman fortress overlooking the city. Amjad Hashem Taki, a captain in the police force, reported in January 2005 that "400 [Sunni] officers . . . quit or joined the insurgency," while noting that US forces were responsible for about 90 percent of all security operations. Another Shiite policeman, Hasanen Khidir, recalled that the insurgents subjected the police to constant small arms and RPG attacks. Surrounded by Sunni Turkmen and terrorized by the insurgents, the Shiite policemen rarely ventured out of the castle, except as death squads to exact retribution through kidnappings, executions, committing "atrocities and injustices," and contributing to a larger "cycle of . . . tribal violence which further destabilized the city and further victimized the people."[13]

Insurgents exploited the thinly spread US forces, making Tall 'Afar the centerpiece in their propaganda campaign following the fall of Fallujah. On a regular basis, their attacks against American patrols and convoys "featured heavily in the 'top 10 attacks' videos circulated among insurgent groups." From May through July 2005, attacks in Tall 'Afar alone accounted for as many as 10 percent of all those in Iraq. Insurgent videos and reports corroborated by residents recounted public executions for those who collaborated with Americans. Had US forces allowed the insurgents

129

to retain control of Tall 'Afar, they would have ceded the initiative to the enemy in northwest Nineveh and handed them an important propaganda victory.[14]

Responding to what had transpired in Tall 'Afar, 2d Squadron shifted northward and established Forward Operating Base (FOB) Sykes at the Tall 'Afar airfield, about 12 kilometers southwest of the city. With Support Squadron under LTC Richard O'Connor sustaining the move and later establishing a detainee screening site south of the city, 2d Squadron prepared the way for the regiment's reception and integration into the new AO, less 3d Squadron, in Operation COLD FUSION (1 May–15 June). While establishing itself in its new AO, the squadron relieved Task Force (TF) 2-14 Cavalry, a Stryker squadron from 1st BCT, 25th Infantry Division, of its responsibility for the province west of Mosul, a brigade-size AO as large as Connecticut. By mid-May, LTC Gregory D. Reilly's 1st Squadron had established itself along the Syrian border, while 4th Squadron, under LTC Douglass Pavek, had shifted to FOB Sykes to conduct operations in Tall 'Afar and western Nineveh. McMaster attempted to have 3d Squadron rejoin the command, but because of mission requirements in Baghdad his attempts proved unsuccessful.[15] (See map 9.)

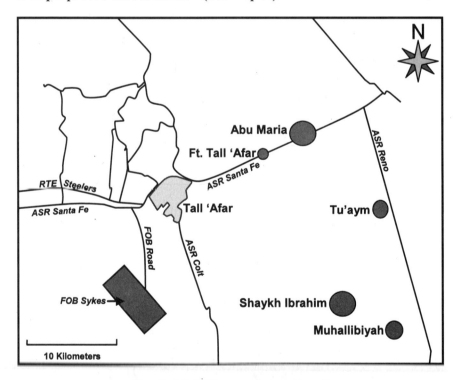

Map 9. 2/3 ACR area of operations.[16]

Partnered with 1st Brigade, 3d Iraqi Division, 2d Squadron initiated an extensive area reconnaissance on arrival in Tall 'Afar. The squadron's operational philosophy, which evolved over the course of its deployment, "followed . . . five tenets . . ., regardless of the level of resistance . . . faced." They were, first, to "Secure the population" by creating and safeguarding an environment in which all Iraqis felt safe and unthreatened by insurgents, thus making the people tacitly, if not overtly, supportive of the counterinsurgency. The second charged Soldiers to "Enable the Iraqi Security Forces" by helping them develop their ability to conduct operations with minimal or no American assistance, an important symbolic and real necessity. Third, "See first, understand first, act decisively." The guidance enjoined troopers to reconnoiter thoroughly and aggressively wherever they operated to develop their situational awareness. It reminded Soldiers to tailor their actions according to the mission's needs, that everything they undertook had immediate and long-term consequences, and that they needed to act quickly to seize and retain the initiative.[17] The fourth tenet directed each trooper to "Understand your unit, its capabilities, and constantly attempt to improve—widen the rumble strips as you go," reducing the need to slow the operational tempo. Finally, this guidance reminded leaders that "Trust and confidence in your subordinates enables initiative—In a counterinsurgency, initiative, speed, agility, and the ability to seize opportunities are critical." These five tenets were not sequential steps; rather they were coterminous.[18]

As the squadron patrolled Tall 'Afar and learned about its new AO, it suffered its first casualties on 28 April when an improvised explosive device (IED) of six or more 122-mm artillery rounds exploded against a Stryker, penetrated its hull, and killed four Soldiers. On 1 May, 2d Squadron assumed full responsibility for operations in and around the city, executing missions designed to develop the squadron's situational awareness through reconnaissance, cordons, searches, and raids. As COLD FUSION commenced, 1st Squadron began its operations along the Syrian border, designed to interdict the flow of foreign fighters and external support while reconstituting the Iraqi border guards.[19]

While 2d Squadron focused on learning its new environment (see map 10), the squadron, along with 1st Brigade, 3d Iraqi Division secured their lines of communication (LOCs) along MSR SANTA FE, and the LOC from FOB Sykes by establishing five Iraqi Army patrol bases to provide overwatch and security. Early on, Hickey realized that the squadron's small number of scouts was not large enough to execute all of the essential dismounted operations required in an urban environment. Responding to Hickey's needs, McMaster requested and received from Task Force

Freedom and Multinational Corps–Iraq (MNC-I), additional dismounted forces. MNC-I responded in time for Operation RESTORING RIGHTS, when it detailed the 4th Police Commando Brigade, a Kurdish *Peshmerga* infantry battalion, and 2-325th Infantry from 2d Brigade, 82d Airborne Division. During this month, insurgents launched 20 IEDs or suicide bomb attacks, 21 mortar or rocket attacks, and 104 attacks with small arms or rocket-propelled grenades (RPGs) against 2d Squadron, residents of the area, and Iraqi security forces. Most of the attacks took place along MSR SANTA FE and against the city's hospital and forces posted to secure it.[20]

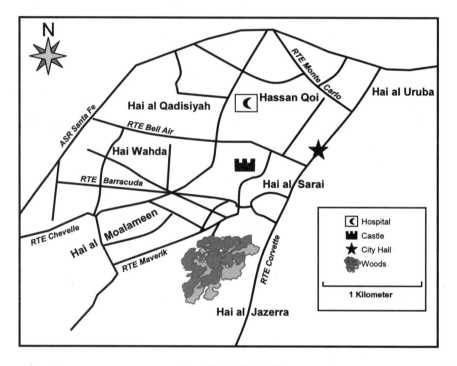

Map 10. *Tall 'Afar.*[21]

On 3 May, G Troop began searching for IEDs in Sarai. Insurgents observed the troop's entry and immediately attacked it with small arms and hand grenades. During the fight, which lasted over 4 hours, the troopers observed women and children being used as shields and children acting as scouts. In the fight, insurgents wounded six Iraqi soldiers. Returning fire and forcing the insurgents to withdraw, the Soldiers secured the area and eventually retired, but they would return 2 days later searching for weapons purportedly stored in a mosque. As Iraqi infantry approached the mosque, insurgents opened fire and inflicted two casualties, which shook the Iraqis' confidence, forcing G Troop's Soldiers to take control of the situation. Stiffened by the American presence, the Iraqis regained their composure and continued fighting as AH64Ds from 4th Squadron supported the attack, which killed 12 insurgents in over 3 hours of combat.[22]

As the squadron continued COLD FUSION, a suicide bomber attacked an E Troop Bradley on 9 May. Because the crew maintained security and fired on the attacker, it prevented the bomber from getting too close. The crew's alertness coupled with the Bradley's armor limited the damage and protected the troopers. It was another 4 months before the insurgents attacked 2d Squadron with a car bomb. In spite of this respite, the insurgents continued their attacks hoping to disrupt American operations and further terrorize and dishearten the Iraqis.[23]

Toward the end of May, the squadron began developing a clearer picture of the situation in Tall 'Afar and the several friction points contributing to the popular alienation that sustained the insurgency. First, the Mounted Riflemen realized the insurgency could not have existed without the tacit support of any number of the 83 sheiks and their tribes, some of which, like the Shiite Sadr and Sunni Farhat, were feuding with one another in the Wahda district. Second, the majority-Shiite police force, when it was not holed up in the castle, was little better than a death squad, spreading its own brand of terror and revenge. The Ministry of the Interior had helped solve this problem in early May when it replaced the corrupt chief, Ferris Ismael, with BG Najim Abdullah al-Jabouri, who later became major of Tall 'Afar. Hickey also suspected the complicity of the mayor, who was able to travel throughout the city with only a small escort while well-armed patrols were regularly attacked. Third, the ill will engendered by Operation BLACK TYPHOON, the uneven progress of rebuilding following that operation, and the 75-percent unemployment rate further contributed to popular discontent. Finally, the largely uneducated or illiterate population was especially susceptible to insurgent suasion. The insurgent centers of gravity in the Sarai and Qadisiyah districts included the city's hospital, itself a frequent target of attacks and attempted seizures by extra-legal security forces. Attacks against what ought to have been a place of healing intensified as Iraqi forces, supported by the squadron, sought to secure it.[24]

On 20 May, 2d Squadron established a cordon around the Qadisiyah district as it executed Operation COLD STEEL, which aimed at killing or capturing insurgents operating in Qadisiyah and demonstrating to them the strength of 2d Squadron's combat power. Operating in conjunction with its Iraqi partner brigade, the squadron captured five suspected insurgents and some weapons. Limited in time, scope, and area when compared to the larger ongoing mission of COLD FUSION, COLD STEEL was the first time Hickey's squadron and its Iraqi partner brigade operated together in a large-scale mission. Hickey anticipated an insurgent reaction; he did not wait long. On the evening of 26 May, over a dozen insurgents, supported by mortars, machine guns, and RPGs, attempted overrunning an Iraqi patrol base in Hassan Qoi. Supported by tanks and a sniper team from H Company, the Iraqis defeated the attempt. In search of easier targets, the insurgents shifted their focus to civilians, hoping to cow them into submission. They miscalculated.[25]

A few days earlier, on 23 May, a suicide car bomber had attacked members of the largely-Shiite Jolaq tribe in retaliation for an earlier attack on two Sunni insurgent leaders, killing 15 and injuring 30. Rather than intimidating the Jolaq, the attack encouraged them to support the counter-insurgency, which created an opportunity for Hickey's troopers to begin earning their trust and further developing their understanding of Tall 'Afar. The improved relations yielded more and better intelligence, which enabled the cavalry troopers to begin seizing more weapons caches, pre-venting more attacks, and gradually building trust with the people.[26]

Throughout June, the squadron executed several squadron-level oper-ations within the city, targeting insurgent safe havens in Hassan Qoi and Sarai. G Troop and Company H supported by the OH58Ds of O Troop, 4th Squadron executed cordon and search missions that seized dozens of weapons, ammunition, and other insurgent materials, while Howitzer Battery became a motorized infantry company and manned traffic control points (TCPs) on the city's outskirts. Despite the squadron's successes and the inroads it had made with some of the populace, Sunnis in eastern Tall 'Afar were reluctant to assist Hickey's men. Their reluctance hampered the squadron's efforts to develop a comprehensive intelligence estimate of the enemy and environment. Based on what information the 2d Squadron was able to gather, the estimate indicated that Hassan Qoi and Sarai con-tinued serving as safe havens for the insurgents and that Qadisiyah was their battleground.[27]

In a 4 June conference with nearly 80 sheiks at Al Kisik, an Iraqi army post about 25 kilometers east-northeast of Tall 'Afar, many of the tribal leaders called for an assault along the lines of the 2004 attack on Falluja to destroy the insurgents. Surprising the American and Iraqi commanders, they complained that US forces were too gentle in their treatment of the insurgents and that the Americans should be rougher on them. American and Iraqi leaders demurred. "Rather than conduct[ing] destructive missions that

134

focused on using an inappropriate amount of firepower," as the squadron's account of its campaign in Tall 'Afar notes, the "Squadron developed the intelligence picture through various reconnaissance operations while simultaneously planning for larger scale operations" that constricted and isolated insurgent safe havens.[28]

Patience and persistence finally paid off when G Troop gained the trust of an informant with a thorough knowledge of the insurgents in Sarai. With the informant's assistance, the squadron began an operation on 7 June that focused on capturing or killing 30 high-value targets (HVTs) in Sarai. The operation detained 23 HVTs "who seemed surprised by the size, timing and direction of the attack from the desert, [and] were caught off guard." Despite the initial surprise, the enemy recovered and fought back, although by the end of the mission they suffered 20 killed and an indeterminate number wounded. In the course of this operation, LTC Terrence Crow of the 98th Advisory Support Team received a mortal wound when the Iraqi soldiers he was leading were ambushed in an alleyway. While en route to the forward aid station, Crow died.[29]

Throughout June, 2d Squadron continued executing cordon and search missions at cavalry-troop level to develop its intelligence picture. By the end of the month, the squadron had come to understand more fully the organization and heterogeneous nature of the insurgency. Acting on this improved understanding, 2d Squadron adjusted its information operations, which were designed to woo the resistance and other Sunni nationalists by stressing that the *Takfiri*, puritanical Sunnis hoping to incite an intra-Islamic civil war, were the common enemy of the Shia and secular Sunni alike. The campaign emphasized that operations were intended to help the Sunnis—not punish them. At the very least, Hickey hoped to avoid alienating the population and creating new enemies. One method in which the squadron underscored its intentions was by treating released detainees with respect and returning them to their homes with cash and new clothes.[30]

The insurgency, 2d Squadron discovered, was anything but monolithic. It was instead a marriage of convenience between disparate, even mutually hostile groups, linked only by a shared antipathy toward Coalition forces and Iraqi collaborators. The first group, known popularly as the "Resistance," was generally comprised of native-born Sunni nationalists fighting for the establishment of a secular Arab nationalist government, similar to a Baathist regime, dominated by Sunnis. Others' motives included "Anger, revenge, economic need, opposition to the US invasion and any government that grows out of it or sheer lack of hope in the current system." Sunni Turkmen nationalists, receiving support from within and outside Iraq, were especially angry because of their perceived exclusion from the political process, their perceived disenfranchisement following the departure of the 101st Airborne from Tall 'Afar in February 2004, their lack of trust in follow-on US and Iraqi forces, and their exclusion from the ranks of the local security forces. Although not easily placated, many of the Turkmen nationalists later proved amenable to American overtures that addressed their concerns.[31]

The other insurgent element facing the Brave Rifles was the intractable group of religiously motivated zealots known as *Takfiri*, adherents of a puritanical strain of Sunni belief, many of whom viewed civil war as a desirable goal in Iraq and throughout the Muslim world. Hoping to create a pure Sunni state free of Jews and Christians, the *Takfiri* deemed it their duty to convert all "apostate" Muslims, or *Kafirs*, to their ways of belief, or barring that to eliminate them. The *Takfiri*, as the Mounted Riflemen discovered, had no compunction about attacking innocent civilians, much less police and soldiers. In their interpretation of struggle, jihad, the *Takfiri* considered civilian sacrifices as justifiable acts committed on behalf of a godly cause. They believed they were doing God's will by fighting a global war on Islamic apostasy.[32]

The *Takfiri* took strength from their conviction that a conventional victory was unnecessary to their cause. A protracted and ever-growing civil war within all Islam, according to their way of thinking, would herald a much larger and welcome conflict signaling the end of the world, an inevitable struggle they believed they would win because God was with them. The insurgency in Tall 'Afar demonstrated in microcosm a greater struggle within Islam and against the American occupation, but also Americans' difficulty in comprehending "an asymmetric war going on within an asymmetric war." As one Iraqi official put it with more than a measure of truth, "'Americans always want one simple enemy. You need to think and act as if you had 250. Some are outsiders, some insiders. Some are fanatics, and some who might be persuaded to join the political process. We have tribes, cells, mosques, towns, and parts of cities with different goals, and different tactics.'"[33]

The 2d Squadron confronted a major dilemma: how best to quash the insurgency while gaining the trust of the people, or, at the very least, not antagonizing them. To unaccustomed American eyes, the insurgents were indistinguishable from the larger population. Their ability to hide in plain sight allowed them to circulate and act with impunity. Without the ability to identify their enemies, American strength and intentions were for naught. So long as the insurgents intimidated the people, the insurgents were safe. Operation BLACK TYPHOON had demonstrated to the people of Tall 'Afar the power of the US Army, but the rapid withdrawal prevented the creation of a safe environment. American forces had killed or driven out insurgents but had then left the people to their own devices, which allowed insurgents to return. How best to render order out of chaos? The squadron could mass its firepower, but where and against whom and to what effect?

*   *   *

Create a safer and more secure environment, Hickey reasoned, and the population would become more amenable to the American presence and more trusting of nascent Iraqi institutions of governance, including the army and police. Working closely with McMaster and regimental planners, Hickey and his staff determined that changing Tall 'Afar's environment would be more productive and result in a longer-lasting effect than focusing on destroying or defeating the insurgents, an impossible task given the squadron's inability to differentiate friends from enemies without local assistance. To accomplish this, the squadron launched a series of shaping and reconnaissance operations that developed its situational awareness, expanded its presence throughout the AO, and made tentative inroads with the population.[34]

Throughout its deployment to Tall 'Afar, the squadron worked at integrating Iraqi forces to improve their operational capabilities and awareness. For most of this period, soldiers of the Iraqi Army's 1st Brigade, 3d Division could only function at squad and lower levels. To raise the Iraqis' proficiency, the squadron increasingly integrated them into operations, with troop commanders partnering with battalion commanders. In spite of their low levels of training, the Iraqis were a valuable source of dismounted infantry for securing routes and protecting fixed structures and sites, as well as for their language skills and understanding of the culture. As 2d Squadron prepared for future operations, it requested additional forces; it received Company D, 1/3 ACR and 3d Battalion, 2d Brigade, 3d Iraqi Division. Elements from Special Forces also arrived to intensify and improve the Iraqis' training and military capacity.[35]

After having developed a clearer picture of the situation in Tall 'Afar, 2d Squadron, joined by 1st Squadron and Special Operations Forces, launched Operation SABRE UNLEASHED (1 July–31 August), a series of shaping operations to create the conditions for Operation RESTORING

RIGHTS—the decisive squadron-level combat operation against the insurgents. In SABRE UNLEASHED, 2d Squadron launched simultaneous attacks throughout the AO that denied the insurgents' freedom of maneuver and significantly disrupted their ability to strike out at Coalition forces and civilians. A crucial element in SABRE UNLEASHED was the positioning of elements from 3d Iraqi Division throughout Tall 'Afar and along the MSR to provide overwatch and security and to deny the insurgents their freedom to maneuver. Nonetheless, the intensity and frequency of insurgent attacks within the city prevented 2d Squadron from positioning Iraqi posts in any appreciable depth.[36]

Because of the scale and scope of this operation, Hickey determined that every mission executed by 2d Squadron elements had the potential to become a squadron-level operation. The degree of communication and resulting situational awareness also enabled troop and company commanders to support one another quickly. According to the squadron's account, "Units became intuitively aware of the actions of adjacent units and became capable of performing outside of their areas in order to provide assistance to other units." On 9 July, a G Troop raid in Sarai turned into a squadron-level operation.[37]

At 0520, G Troop executed a raid in search of surface-to-air missiles. Serving alongside G Troop were Special Forces teams partnered with the Iraqi 3d Battalion, 1st Brigade, and O and P Troops from 4th Squadron. Air Force close air support (CAS) and OH58D crews from O Troop reported on suspicious actions in the area, which alerted G Troop to establish a cordon around it. Dismounted cavalrymen initiated the search of a suspected house and began receiving fire from insurgents. G Troop expanded the search to other houses and began securing the area. The fight expanded as insurgents opened fire with RPGs on a tank platoon as it began securing a school, key terrain in the neighborhood. In response, O Troop shifted to provide CAS as elements from F Troop moved in to assist while G Troop conducted a casualty evacuation (CASEVAC) for a wounded Soldier, SPC Hoby Bradfield. Finally securing the area, the search uncovered insurgent propaganda CDs, RPG warheads, a suicide-bomb vest, and other weapons. At 0540 the M113 ambulance carrying the wounded Soldier struck an IED, which destroyed it, killed one medic, and wounded another; doctors with the 228th Combat Surgical Hospital in Mosul pronounced Bradfield dead. The blast site, which was under observation by insurgents, grew into a firefight as elements from F Troop secured the area.[38]

G Troop's battle continued to grow, drawing in more participants from throughout the squadron. As a psychological operations (PSYOP) team

138

broadcast messages from the castle, tanks from E Troop made their way to support G Troop, which was returning fire with 120-mm main gun, 25-mm chain-gun, machine gun, and M136 AT4 antitank fire. Insurgent sniper, small arms, and RPG fire continued as Special Forces and Iraqi soldiers joined in the fight with 40-mm grenade fire. Throughout the fight, H Company provided overwatch and engaged with main gun fire insurgents who were harassing retiring units. The mission ended later that morning with six detainees in hand.[39]

Shortly after the Sarai raid, surveillance imagery identified insurgents planting IEDs on the city's east side. The squadron also received information from residents about an insurgent IED class being held. Howitzer Battery, at FOB Sykes, opened up with its 155-mm guns, which cancelled class. This sort of activity continued over the next 48 hours, and each time Howitzer Battery responded. The squadron received reports that its fire killed over 30 and wounded another 20 insurgents.

Searches and raids continued throughout the shaping operation. In July, the squadron learned of booby-trapped houses in Qadisiyah and accompanying insurgent activity that was believed to be an attempt to divert the squadron's attention from Sarai. Responding to this information, Hickey launched a squadron-level raid against a dozen or so targets in Qadisiyah on 30 July, capturing 24 insurgents.[40]

Learning that the forest on the city's southeastern edge was a source for cached insurgent supplies, 2d Squadron launched an extensive reconnaissance of the woods and the nearby neighborhoods on 7 August. The mission began with a 65-round artillery barrage at 0445, as P Troop established overwatch and maintained aerial security. After uncovering several caches and killing, capturing, or wounding a number of insurgents, the squadron notified the city that the forest was off limits. It also declared the woods a "free fire" zone.[41]

In an attempt to disrupt the flow of insurgent supplies, the squadron executed several operations in locations outside of Tall 'Afar, including transit and supply points within Muhalibiya and Sheik Ibrahim. From 18 to 26 July, 1st Squadron reinforced 2d Squadron's efforts when it deployed half of its strength to Avgani, about 15 kilometers north of Tall 'Afar. Participation by 1st Squadron in this operation and the following operation (23 August–23 September) was significant to the outcome, but the "opportunity cost in this was halting all border defense force training and interdictions along the Iraq/Syrian border, [actions] which GEN [George] Casey . . . [had deemed] operationally significant." After weighing the decision to deploy 1st Squadron to Tall 'Afar, McMaster decided it was worth the risk. On the cusp of Operation RESTORING RIGHTS, US and Iraqi forces massed some 3,000 US Soldiers and 5,500 Iraqi soldiers and police, bringing the troop-to-civilian ratio to something between 1:23 and 1:17.[42]

With much of the regiment's strength concentrated in the Tall 'Afar AO, American forces began constructing a 12-kilometer berm around Tall 'Afar to control traffic in and out of the city and to deny insurgents their freedom to maneuver. The suggestion to build the berm may have come from Mayor Najim Abdullah al-Jabouri, who was then commanding Tall 'Afar's police, and MG Khorsheed Saleem al-Dosekey, commander of the Iraqi 3d Division. Najim and Khorsheed believed that the berm's real value was the psychological impact it would have on the insurgents, visually and mentally constricting their ability to maneuver. As with other obstacles, the berm's effectiveness would depend on the degree to which US and Iraqi forces observed and covered it with direct and indirect fire. This obstacle was reminiscent of recent barriers built by US forces in Iraq: in 2005 Army engineers built a 64-kilometer berm around Mosul, in 2004 US forces encircled Fallujah with an earthen berm, and in 2003 an infantry battalion "wrapped" the village of Abu Hishma in concertina wire. From within Tall 'Afar, thousands of people vacated the city as US forces built the berm and publicly announced the coming offensive; the magnitude of the exodus and ability and process in determining whether those fleeing were insurgents or innocents may have been problematic. Insurgents fled alongside the innocent, but in doing so removed themselves from play and were thus unable to continue terrorizing the city. In order to ease the straits of Tall 'Afar's evacuees, Support Squadron established a center for displaced Iraqis that provided food and shelter for over 1,500 people.[43]

As SABRE UNLEASHED approached its final stages, Sunni tribal leaders inclined toward the insurgency in Tall 'Afar pressed the government in Baghdad for relief from American operations while their Shiite peers called for a military solution along the lines of Operation PHANTOM FURY. By the close of August, 2d Squadron had executed over 1,500 reconnaissance patrols, 111 cordons and searches, and 46 raids. It had also destroyed over 900 enemy weapons, including artillery pieces and assorted munitions, captured over 200 insurgents or suspected insurgents, and killed over 130.[44]

In preparation for Operation RESTORING RIGHTS, the Regiment of Mounted Rifles massed "well over 3,000 [US] Soldiers" and 5,500 Iraqi soldiers and police, including the Shiite "Wolf" Brigade, a police commando unit. The regiment's "main effort" was 2d Squadron as 1st Squadron and 3d Brigade, 3d Iraqi Division assumed responsibility for the western half of the city. Hickey's scheme of maneuver sent E Troop, Company H, and two Iraqi battalions southward through Sarai, as F and G Troops, with Company A, 113th Combat Engineers, and three Iraqi battalions advanced to the north. Save a predetermined route to the south, the concentration of American and Iraqi forces in Sarai, the berm to the east, and 1st Squadron and its Iraqi partner brigade to the west was supposed to have effectively sealed the district. Throughout the course of the zone reconnaissance, insurgent isolation, and deliberate attacks, US forces publicly announced their intentions, allowing innocents and insurgents to flee or shift positions. Hickey aimed to drive the insurgents, along with the remaining civilians, through the opening as his forces executed a zone reconnaissance. He found himself commanding more Soldiers than were in most brigades; his captains commanding the equivalent of battalions.[45]

The operation commenced on 2 September with a "3-day zone reconnaissance." PSYOP teams broadcast orders forbidding digging and the carrying of weapons. Coalition forces encountered heavy resistance in the south, but only infrequent sniper fire to the north. An Avenger platoon from the regiment's ADA Battery established an overwatch position on the eastern edge of the city, and Special Operations Forces set up blocking positions at the castle to prevent movement to the west. By the end of the day, the 2d Squadron had established patrol bases as it prepared for deliberate attacks the next day. Some of Tall 'Afar's citizens began to come forward and volunteer information on the whereabouts of the enemy, their strength, and identities. The second day's operations began early the next morning, but with much less resistance; some Soldiers expressed wonderment at this turn of events. Most of the engagements that did take place involved suppressing enemy fire, cordoning off buildings, and searching them. In some cases, insurgents abandoned their weapons and started withdrawing deeper into the city, hoping to blend with the population and eventually escape.[46]

The third day of the operation, 4 September, resistance intensified. Withdrawing insurgents had booby-trapped houses. Engaging the enemy with 120-mm tank main guns, 25-mm Bradley chain guns, 30-mm Apache guns, TOWs, Hellfires, and .50-caliber and coaxial machine gun fire, 2d Squadron, supported by R Troop, 4th Squadron, drove deeper into Sarai; dismounted troopers and Iraqi soldiers cleared houses, even using sledgehammers to break down doors. Aviation elements "found themselves, at times, firing within 50–75 meters of friendly . . . forces." By the end of the day, Coalition forces had reached the limits of their advance, Phase Lines (Routes) BELL AIR and BARRACUDA; they then prepared for the evacuation of Sarai.[47]

Originally, the evacuation was to have lasted 3 days; instead, on the orders of Prime Minister Ibrahim al-Jafaari, it lasted a week. Insurgents attempted their escapes by mixing with civilians. Five insurgents dressed as women, including one with false breasts, were detained at a checkpoint. Others grasped children's hands, hoping to insinuate themselves into families and facilitate their escape. In 1st Squadron's AOR, the Shiite 4th Commando Brigade, the self-proclaimed "Wolf Brigade" returned to Tall 'Afar. Still poorly disciplined and ill-trained, it had been selected by the Interior Ministry over the more experienced 1st Brigade, which was commanded by a Sunni Turkmen. The Wolves' deployment was short-lived—senior US commanders requested its immediate withdrawal because of its low level of training, poor discipline, and concerns from the Sunni population. In these final stages of the operation, one intelligence officer noted that "al-Qaeda is slipping to the east and behind them to the south, and 'somehow—we don't know how'—cutting through the screen line to . . . the west," and across the berm.[48]

According to *Time* reporter Michael Ware, the delay left American Soldiers frustrated, angry, and "embittered." A Special Forces sergeant decried the pause as a "'goat f___.'" When the final assault began, "Not a hostile shot" was fired, nor were any insurgents found. According to Ware, "Only one blackened corpse, left rotting for days, [was] found. 'They've even removed their dead,' said a Green Beret, not really believing it himself." This NCO had but a limited view of the operation. Assigned to an Iraqi battalion from Irbil, about 150 kilometers to the east, he was unaware of the fuller details of Operation RESTORING RIGHTS and the emphasis on creating a secure environment over simply killing insurgents. Nonetheless, the regiment had killed over 150 and detained some 600, although a number of the detainees were released for lack of evidence or because of false accusations.[49]

On 14 September, after having cleared Sarai, 2d Squadron temporarily handed it and Hassan Qoi over to the control of LTC Christopher Gibson's 2-325 Infantry. This freed 2d Squadron to secure the populace and lay the groundwork for Tall 'Afar's reconstruction and recovery, and to prepare it for the constitutional referendum on 15 October 2005. Two days later, on 16 September, 1st Squadron began its return to the Sinjar area along the Iraqi-Syrian border. Hickey now faced a second major decision. In September 2004, following the conclusion of Operation BLACK TYPHOON, Ham had decided to pull American forces out of Tall 'Afar. The withdrawal recognized the realities of the situation: there were not enough American forces to maintain order and oversee Tall 'Afar's reconstruction while other parts of Iraq begged for the deployment of American troops. Moreover, the need to foster a positive image of American forces as allies rather than as occupiers demanded that US forces turn over responsibility to Iraqi security forces. The level of American forces in 2005 was not appreciably different from that in 2004. Thus, Hickey's dilemma was similar to the one Ham faced in the aftermath of BLACK TYPHOON. On the one hand, retiring from the city would have been an invitation for the return of the insurgents and an important propaganda victory for their cause. On the other hand, should the squadron stay, it risked giving the impression to the Iraqis that it was an occupying force.[50]

        *   *   *

Hickey elected to stay; it was a decision that had developed out of the squadron's experience in Tall 'Afar and in the aftermath of BLACK TYPHOON. Rather than operating from FOB Sykes, the squadron established or expanded its TCPs and troop-size patrol bases throughout the city. From this point forward, 2d Squadron remained in Tall 'Afar. As Iraqi security forces grew and developed their proficiency, the scale and depth of the security penetration increased. Because of the castle's symbolic importance to the people, Hickey shifted squadron headquarters to the old fortress and collocated with the city's police headquarters and the headquarters of the Iraqi 1st Brigade, 3d Division. The collocated headquarters led to the establishment of a joint operations center (JOC) in the castle. With civil, military, police, fire, and power representatives staffing it, the JOC served as a central collection and action point for intelligence, operations, education, and training. The new locations allowed the squadron to execute its missions more rapidly as it continued hunting down insurgents. It also offered improved access for citizens willing to share information. While the shift took place, many of the insurgents remaining within the city attempted their escapes, often adopting the guises of women, ambulance drivers, and family members. Yet others continued trying to place IEDs.[51]

With US control established and insurgent operations disrupted, the squadron now directed the delivery of food, water, and other necessities. Iraqi soldiers met returning citizens to develop a rapport and good will with the people, but also to screen the people while looking for insurgents. These soldiers also informed the people of the processes for initiating claims for damages. Hickey and the Iraqi leadership initiated information operations (IO) to appeal to the Sunni population to join the political and reconstruction processes and to enlist in the local security forces.[52]

Throughout October, the remaining insurgents attempted to reestablish their bases in the city to disrupt the constitutional referendum and demonstrate their resilience. US and Iraqi forces seized a number of AK47s, sniper rifles, an IED, 60-mm mortar rounds, binoculars, and four suspected insurgents on 4 October 2005 in Qadisiyah. In spite of the insurgents' best attempts at reestablishing themselves in Tall 'Afar, the tempo of operations had clearly changed. Missions were still combat missions, but the size of the squadron's elements was scaled back from platoon to squad and even section level. The smaller patrols gave the Brave Rifles a wider geographic presence and enabled them to work more closely with the Iraqi units. As Iraqi proficiency and confidence grew, so too did their ability to begin working autonomously. The changes allowed the squadron to increase its presence by establishing platoon-size patrol bases throughout the city.[53]

As units became more familiar with problem areas, they began positioning security forces and altering patrol routes to address the grievances of the population. Troops began to establish platoon-size patrol bases in and around Tall 'Afar. Likewise, the Iraqi army began to position itself within the AO to provide constant security to more citizens simultaneously. As the US–Iraqi presence expanded, so too did the number of residents returning to their neighborhoods. Potential recruits also began reporting to the police recruiting station in the castle, with some 300 the first 2 days alone. The squadron estimated that 60 to 70 percent were Sunni. In the end, the squadron aimed at establishing a force of 1,480.[54]

In addition to its security mission, the squadron oversaw reconstruction and other civil-military operations, including restoring critical services like water, power, medical services, and the school system. Civil Affairs teams "managed over $4 million in projects designed to restore life to the city and address the long-term grievances of the population." Within the castle, the squadron also established a civil-military operations center for handling civilian claims for damages, bidding on construction projects, searching for missing relatives, and an employment center. A government support team, also manned by Civil Affairs Soldiers, leant a hand to Tall 'Afar's city council as it established procedures for daily affairs and the functioning of firefighting and rescue, power, and communications. To hasten the city's economic recovery, the squadron disbursed compensatory funds to people whose property had been damaged. A few weeks later, the Iraqi government authorized paying 150,000 dinars, roughly $100, per family as compensation for damage resulting from Operation RESTORING RIGHTS. In the end, Iraqi army and police disbursed roughly 4.5 billion dinars.[55]

With the 15 October referendum approaching, the squadron, like other US and Coalition units, created election sites. Security was provided by the 3d Iraqi Division's 1st Brigade as 2d Squadron stood back and provided a quick reaction force should trouble develop. Security procedures, preparations, troop dispositions, screening sites, voter and crowd control, and the management of the 11 polling stations was left to the Iraqi government and security forces. In the days approaching the referendum, insurgents launched attacks against the people in an attempt to dissuade them from voting; two of the attacks were directed at police recruits. In each of these cases, Iraqi forces had secured the sites and taken control of the situation before cavalry troopers arrived.[56]

On the day of the referendum, an estimated 17,000 people voted in Tall 'Afar, a 1,700 percent increase from the 1,000 or so who had voted in the January 2005 elections. US and Iraqi forces had disrupted the insurgency, but they had not completely ended insurgent activity. On 16 October, Company H uncovered the second-largest cache discovered during the squadron's deployment. In Muhalibiya the tankers discovered more than 30 120-mm mortar rounds, 95 155-mm artillery rounds, 50 120-mm warheads, and numerous other munitions. On 20 October, F Troop discovered a suicide car bomb in the final stages of construction, with "detonating cord running into the hood and hasty wiring in the seat."[57]

To extend its control in the city, Hickey's squadron threw up barriers to regulate movement and limit the insurgents' freedom to maneuver. It limited access to secondary roads by establishing TCPs at major intersections, "blocking lateral routes throughout the area," and along suspected insurgent avenues of approach. Second Squadron integrated these static measures within an active plan that established a fuller depth of observation throughout the city. In June, insurgent attacks had averaged six per day, by the end of October they had decreased to just over two per day, and in November averaged less than one attack per day.[58]

Throughout November, Howitzer Battery and Iraqi authorities bolstered Tall 'Afar's police by recruiting over 1,000 new police officers and building or rehabilitating 4 police stations. Recruits received their training at the Jordanian Iraqi Police Academy or the Mosul Police and Security Academy. The squadron improved its Iraqi partnerships by integrating the expanded and now better-trained police force within its operations. To further enhance coordination and security, and strengthen the links between US and Iraqi forces, the Mounted Riflemen and their Iraqi partners exchanged company and troop-level liaison officers. The squadron also held weekly security meetings at the JOC with Iraqi battalion commanders, police station chiefs, and squadron troop commanders, and realigned police boundaries with military boundaries. US and Iraqi forces continued targeting the troublesome Hai al-Wahda and Qadisiyah neighborhoods in joint operations, which typically included a cavalry troop, an Iraqi battalion, and a company from the 2-325th Infantry.[59]

The squadron's last large-scale operation took place on 4 December in Qadisiyah. Concentrating D, E, and F Troops, the squadron launched a zone reconnaissance to identify, detain, or kill insurgents. Breaking with past operations, much of the planning responsibility devolved to Iraqi army and police commanders; the intent was to screen every military-aged male (MAM) in the area. Starting in the middle of Tall 'Afar and pushing north, Hickey's intent was to drive insurgents into northern Qadisiyah, which would be cordoned off by E and F Troops. Iraqi forces rounded up and screened over 800 MAMs, 93 of whom were detained. About 40 of the 93 were sent on to Abu Ghraib for further interrogation. Following this operation, insurgent attacks were less destructive, less lethal, and seemed to be less coordinated. December attacks dropped to less than one per day.[60]

As the situation in Tall 'Afar evolved, so too did the nature of 2d Squadron's operations in the city. Assigning 2-325th Infantry the responsibility for Sarai freed the squadron's troop and company commanders to execute independent operations within their areas of responsibility. With growing frequency, Iraqi companies and platoons began executing searches and raids with more autonomy. Civil affairs and Iraqi government projects pumped over $60 million into infrastructure improvements and repairs. Other positive indications included regular police patrols and investigations, a functioning court system, and signs of the return of economic life.[61]

On 15 December, Iraq held national elections. As in October, the squadron provided logistical support and prepared to support Iraqi security forces. Increased turnout by Sunnis forced the squadron to establish and even man polling sites. Over 40,000 Iraqis cast votes in Tall 'Afar, with an additional 30,000 doing so in the rest of the squadron's AO. The event was marred when insurgents fired about four 60-mm rounds, which killed two children and wounded four. Shortly after the elections, 2-325th Infantry departed. To help make up for its departure and maintain a presence in Sarai, the regiment's 43d Combat Engineer Company assumed responsibility for a portion of the neighborhood. Other shifts took place in the Tall 'Afar AO. On 6 January 2006, 1st Brigade, 3d Iraqi Division moved just north of Tall 'Afar to reconstitute; it was replaced by the division's 2d Brigade. Finally, Company H, along with the 1st Battalion, 2d

Iraqi Brigade, established a patrol base in Muhalibiya on 21 January to interdict insurgent traffic.[62]

The Brave Rifles transferred authority for western Nineveh to 1st BCT, 1st Armored Division on 19 February 2006. The unit most responsible for Tall 'Afar, the 2d Squadron, lost 8 of its troopers along with another 12 Soldiers serving alongside the cavalrymen. A total of 59 Soldiers received the Purple Heart. One Soldier was decorated with the Silver Star, 28 received the Bronze Star with V device, 72 received the Army Commendation Medals with V devices, and 740 received the Combat Action, Combat Infantry, or Combat Medical Badges. Thirty-eight Iraqi soldiers were killed and 15 wounded; insurgents killed 6 Tall 'Afar policemen and wounded 24. On 4 September 2006, a year after the start of Operation RESTORING RIGHTS, the Federal News Service noted that "all of the Iraqi Army battalions in Tal Afar have taken the lead in security operations." There was no standard solution by which 2d Squadron accomplished its mission in Tall 'Afar. Overwhelming firepower enabled the squadron to defeat the insurgents militarily, and an especially high troop density allowed it to secure Tall 'Afar, gain the people's trust, and set the stage for the city's reconstruction. Whether that degree of success can be replicated remains to be seen.[63]

Notes

1. The 3d ACR was organized as the Regiment of Mounted Riflemen in 1846; it was redesignated as the 3d Cavalry in 1861. Redesignated as the 3d Cavalry Group in 1943, the regiment was finally designated as the 3d Armored Cavalry Regiment in 1948. Department of the Army, *Blood and Steel! The History, Customs, and Traditions of the 3d Armored Cavalry Regiment* (Fort Carson, CO: Office of Historical Programs, Third Cavalry Museum, Fort Carson, CO, 2002), online at <http://www.carson.army.mil/UNITS/3RD%20ACR/main%20pages/3d%20ACR%20History.pdf>, 61–62, accessed September 2006; The 3d Armored Cavalry Regiment in Operation Iraqi Freedom-III, Headquarters, 3d Armored Cavalry Regiment, Fort Carson, CO, online at <http://www.carson.army.mil/UNITS/3RD%20ACR/main%20pages/docs/3d%20ACR%20in%20OIF%20III%20-%20Media%20File.pdf>, accessed August 2006; Michael Simmering, Memorandum for Record, 2/3 ACR Actions During Operation Iraqi Freedom (OIF 04–06), 30 January 2006, 2; LTC Ross Brown, 3/3 ACR Operations and Intelligence Briefing, 21 September 2006, School for Command Preparation, Fort Leavenworth, KS; LTC Gregory D. Reilly, interview by Operational Leadership Experiences (OLE) Project Team, Combat Studies Institute, digital recording, 31 August 2006, Fort Leavenworth, KS [digital recording stored on CD-ROM at Combined Arms Research Library, Fort Leavenworth, KS]; Regimental Education: Brave Rifles Reading List for Operation Iraqi Freedom, 1 November 2004; 3d Squadron, 3d Armored Cavalry Regiment, Thunder Squadron, "Squadron After Action Review: OIF 04–06 January 2005–February 2006," 4-8, 5-5, 6-6, 8-4–5.

2. 3d Armored Cavalry Regiment in Operation Iraqi Freedom-III; Simmering, 2/3 ACR Actions, 2; Brown, 3/3 ACR Operations and Intelligence Briefing; Reilly interview; 3/3 AAR. While 2d Squadron was 3d ACR's main effort in Tall 'Afar and the squadron is the focus of this study, the broader concept, scope, execution, and outcome of the undertaking were regimental operations; e-mail from MAJ Robert J. Molinari to LTC Keith A. Barclay, 2 November 2006, in author's collection.

3. Brown, 3/3 ACR Operations and Intelligence Briefing; the 571st Medical did not deploy with the regiment, but insetad supported III Marine Expeditionary Force out of Al Asad Airfield, in western Iraq's Anbar province; Molinari e-mail to Barclay.

4. Simmering, 2/3 ACR Actions, 2; LTC Christopher M. Hickey, interview by Operational Leadership Experiences (OLE) Project Team, Combat Studies Institute, digital recording, 10 August 2006, Fort Leavenworth, KS [digital recording stored on CD-ROM at Combined Arms Research Library, Fort Leavenworth, KS]; 3d Armored Cavalry Regiment in Operation Iraqi Freedom-III; Simmering, 2/3 ACR Actions, 2; Hickey interview; Michael Ware, "Chasing the Ghosts," *Time*, 26 September 2005, 166: 13, online at <http://www.time.com/time/magazine/article/0,9171,1106333,00.html>, accessed August 2006; Initial Impressions Report: 3d ACR OIF Post Deployment AAR Process IIR, 6–25 (Fort Leavenworth, KS:

Center for Army Lessons Learned, 2006), 31; Brown, 3/3 ACR Operations and Intelligence Briefing.

5. Steve Fainaru, "After Recapturing N. Iraqi City, Rebuilding Starts from Scratch," *Washington Post,* 19 September 2004; George Packer, "Letter from Iraq: The Lesson of Tal Afar," *The New Yorker,* vol. 86 (April 2006), 5; Simmering, 2/3 ACR Actions, 4; GlobalSecurity.org, online at <http://www.globalsecurity.org/military/world/iraq/tall-afar.htm>, <http://www.globalsecurity.org/military/ops/oif-restoring-rights.htm>, accessed August 2006; LTC Paul Yingling, interview by Operational Leadership Experiences (OLE) Project Team, Combat Studies Institute, digital recording, 22 September 2006, Fort Leavenworth, KS [digital recording stored on CD-ROM at Combined Arms Research Library, Fort Leavenworth, KS]; Structure of the Tall Afar Insurgency, 3d ACR File, communication from Patrick R. Jennings, 126th Military History Detachment, Massachusetts Army National Guard, in author's collection.

6. Simmering, 2/3 ACR Actions, 4; LTC Christopher M. Hickey, conversation with author, 26 September 2006.

7. Fainaru, "Rebuilding Starts From Scratch"; Packer, 5; Simmering, 2/3 ACR Actions, 4; GlobalSecurity.org; Structure of the Tall Afar Insurgency, Anthony Cordesman, "New Patterns in the Iraqi Insurgency: The War for a Civil War in Iraq" (Washington, DC: Center for Strategic and International Studies, working draft, rev. 27 September 2005), 1–3; Yingling interview; Michael Knights, "Northern Iraq Faces Increased Instability in 2005," *Janes Intelligence Review,* February 2005, 30.

8. Packer, 2, 5; Richard A. Oppel, Jr., "Magnet for Iraq Insurgents is Test for U.S. Strategy," *New York Times,* 16 June 2005.

9. Packer, 2; David Pratt, "The Battle to Control the Streets of Tal Afar, Iraq: Purging the Insurgents," *Sunday Herald* (Glasgow), 1 January 2006; Cordesman, "War for a Civil War," 28.

10. Packer, 1; Pratt, "Streets of Tal Afar"; GlobalSecurity.Com, "Operation Black Typhoon," online at <http://www.globalsecurity.org/military/ops/oif-black-typhoon.htm>, accessed August 2006; Fainaru, "Rebuilding Starts From Scratch"; id., "U.S.-Led Forces Retake Northern Iraqi City," *Washington Post,* 13 September 2004; Ann Scott Tyson, "Ten Days in Tall Afar; An Exception, Not a Model that is Easily Replicated," *Washington Post,* 26 March 2006; Yingling interview.

11. Packer, "Letter from Iraq," 1; Pratt, "Streets of Tal Afar"; GlobalSecurity. Com, "Operation Black Typhoon"; Fainaru, "Rebuilding Starts From Scratch"; id., "Forces Retake Northern Iraqi City"; Jonathan Finer, "5,000 U.S. and Iraqi Troops Sweep into City of Tall Afar; Urban Assault is Largest Since Last Year," *Washington Post,* 3 September 2005; Oppel, "Magnet for Iraq Insurgents."

12. Finer, "Troops Sweep into City of Tall Afar"; Edward Wong, "Raids in Mosul Region Undermine Value of Victories," *New York Times,* 15 November 2004; Knights, "Increased Instability," 31; Tyson, "Ten Days in Tall Afar"; Simmering, 2/3 ACR Actions, 3.

13. COL H.R. McMaster, interview for Frontline, "The Insurgency," Public Broadcasting System (fall 2005); Charles Crain, "Iraq's New Cops, Under Fire," *Time* 165, no. 5 (31 January 2005), 37; Pratt, "Purging the Insurgents"; Packer, "Letter from Iraq," 5.

14. Ware, "Chasing the Ghosts."

15. Ibid.; Brown, 3/3 ACR Operations and Intelligence Briefing; Molinari e-mail to Barclay.

16. Simmering, 2/3 ACR Actions, 7.

17. Ibid., 6; Hickey interview.

18. Simmering, 2/3 ACR Actions, 6; Hickey interview.

19. Simmering, 2/3 ACR Actions, 8–9.

20. Ibid; Molinari e-mail to Barclay.

21. Simmering, 2/3 ACR Actions, 7.

22. Ibid., 10.

23. Ibid.

24. Simmering, 2/3 ACR Actions, 9–13; Hickey interview; Squadron Commanding Officer's Counterinsurgency Operation Briefing, "2nd Squadron, 3d ACR: Fighting the Insurgency in Tall Afar," version 1, 2006; Finer, "Troops Sweep into City of Tall Afar"; Lawrence F. Kaplan, "The Case for Staying in Iraq: Centripetal Force," *The New Republic*, 6 March 2006, 22; LTC Paul Yingling, personal e-mail message, 23 June 2006.

25. Simmering, 2/3 ACR Actions, 12; Christopher M. Hickey, "Sabre Squadron," *Mounted Rifleman,* May 2005, 12.

26. Simmering, 2/3 ACR Actions, 12–13, 17.

27. Ibid., 14–15.

28. Simmering, 2/3 ACR Actions, 11; Oppel, "Magnet for Iraq Insurgents"; SFC Donald Sparks, "Conference Focuses on Security for Tall Afar," *Mounted Rifleman,* June 2005, 7.

29. Ibid., 15–17; Yingling interview; Richard A. Oppel, Jr., "Dozens Seized in Dawn Raid in Iraq's North," *New York Times,* 8 June 2006.

30. Simmering, 2/3 ACR Actions, 23; Hickey interview.

31. Cordesman, "War for a Civil War," 1; Simmering, 2/3 ACR Actions, 1, 2, 5; Hickey interview.

32. Cordesman, "War for a Civil War," 1; Simmering, 2/3 ACR Actions, 1, 2, 5; Hickey interview.

33. Cordesman, "War for a Civil War," 3, 1; Finer, "Few Foreigners Are Found."

34. Hickey conversation.

35. Simmering, 2/3 ACR Actions, 22.

36. Ibid., 24.

37. Ibid., 25.

38. Ibid., 25–26.

39. Ibid.

40. Ibid., 27.

41. Simmering, 2/3 ACR Actions, 24–31; Jonathan Finer, "U.S. Troops

Cordon Part of Iraqi Town to Trap Insurgents: Rebels Have Fled Undetected in the Past," *Washington Post,* 5 September 2005.

42. Simmering, 2/3 ACR Actions, 24–31; Reilly interview. The ratio is premised on a population of between 200,000 and 150,000. In the case of 8,800 Soldiers, the ratio works out to between 1:23 and 1:17. Some estimates of troop strength have ranged from as low as 6,000 to as high as 11,000, bringing the Soldier-to-civilian ratio to something between 1:33 and 1:13; Yingling interview; Hickey conversation; Frederick W. Kagan, "A Plan for Victory in Iraq: Defeat the Insurgents Militarily—Here's How," *The Weekly Standard,* vol. 11: 35 (29 May 2006), 5; Packer, 3; Kaplan, "Case for Staying in Iraq," 23; Initial Impressions Report, 34–35; Molinari e-mail to Barclay.

43. Simmering, 2/3 ACR Actions, 24; Hickey conversation. Some accounts claim the berm was as large as 80 kilometers. Finer, "U.S. Troops Cordon Part of Iraqi Town"; id., "As Offensive in Iraq Continues, Troops Find Unexpected Quiet," *Washington Post* (12 September 2005); Yingling interview; Michael Gilbert, "Soldiers of (Good) Fortune: Strykers Find Weapons Cache," (Tacoma) *News Tribune,* 19 July 2005; Bing West, "In Fallujah, Resistance Is Futile," *Slate,* 23 May 2006, online at <http://www.slate.com/id/2142009/>, accessed September 2006; Dexter Filkins, "Tough New Tactics by U.S. Tighten Grip on Iraq Town," *New York Times,* 7 December 2003; Molinari e-mail to Barclay.

44. Simmering, 2/3 ACR Actions, 30–31.

45. Ibid., 32–39; Hickey interview; Brown, 3/3 ACR Operations and Intelligence Briefing.

46. Simmering, 2/3 ACR Actions, 32–39; Jonathan Finer, "U.S.-Led Assault in N. Iraq Town Meets Little Insurgent Resistance," *Washington Post,* 4 September 2005.

47. Simmering, 2/3 ACR Actions, 32–39; After Action Review, 4th Commando Brigade Deployment to Tall Afar, Headquarters, 2d Brigade, 75th Division, Special Police Commando Division Transition Team, 21 September 2005; Finer, "U.S. Troops Cordon Part of Iraqi Town."

48. Ware, "Chasing the Ghosts"; Yingling interview.

49. Ware, "Chasing the Ghosts"; Oppel, "Under Pressure, Rebels Abandon an Iraqi Stronghold," *New York Times,* 12 September 2005; 4th CDO Bde AAR; Simmering, 2/3 ACR Actions, 39.

50. Simmering, 2/3 ACR Actions, 38–39; John J. McGrath, *Boots on the Ground: Troop Density in Contingency Operations* (Fort Leavenworth, KS: Combat Studies Institute Press, 2006), 165.

51. Simmering, 2/3 ACR Actions, 39, 45.

52. Ibid.

53. Ibid., 39.

54. Ibid., 41, 46; Hickey interview. The Iraqi payment periods were 30 October–1 November and 19–20 November 2005.

55. Simmering, 2/3 ACR Actions, 42–43.

56. Ibid., 43–44.

57. Ibid., 44–45.

58. Ibid., 46.

59. Ibid., 47. By 1 December over 1,746 recruits were in training.

60. Ibid., 48–49.

61. Ibid., 49.

62. Ibid., 49–51.

63. Ibid., 51; U.S. Federal News Service, "IA Takes Lead Security Role in Tal Afar," 4 September 2006; Sabrina Tavernise, "Suicide Bomber Kills 17 in a Shiite Marketplace in Northern Iraq," *New York Times,* 10 May 2006; Oppel and Abdul Razzaq al-Saiedi, "Suicide Bombers Kill at Least 23 in Iraq," *New York Times*, 10 May 2006.

Glossary

1 MAR DIV	1st Marine Division
1LT	first lieutenant
2LT	second lieutenant
AAFES	Army and Air Force Exchange Service
AAR	after action review
ACE	armored combat earthmover
ACM	anticoalition militia
ACR	armored cavalry regiment
ADA	air defense artillery
AIF	Anti-Iraqi Forces
ANA	Afghan National Army
AO	area of operations
AR	Armor Regiment
ARCENT	Army Central Command
ARCOM-V	Army Commendation Medal with Valor Distinction
ASF	Afghan Special Forces
ASR	ammunition supply route
ATV	all-terrain vehicle
BCT	brigade combat team
BFV	Bradley Fighting Vehicle
BG	brigadier general
bn	battalion
BRT	brigade reconnaissance team
C2	command and control
CAS	close air support
CASEVAC	casualty evacuation
CCP	casualty collection point
CD	compact disc
CFLCC	Coalition Forces Land Component Command
CJSOTF	Combined Joint Special Operations Task Force
CMO	civil-military operations
CNN	Cable News Network
COL	colonel
COP	Combat Outpost
CP	checkpoint
CPATT	Civilian Police Assistance Training Team
CPT	captain
CSI	Combat Studies Institute
CSM	command sergeant major
DVIDS	Digital Video and Imagery Distribution System
E5	sergeant
EN	Engineer
etc.	et cetera (and so forth)

ETT	Embedded Training Team
FA	Field Artillery
FOB	forward operating base
FRE	former regime element
GEN	general
GMV	ground mobility vehicles
GWOT	Global War on Terrorism
HHC	headquarters and headquarters company
HMMWV	high-mobility multipurpose wheeled vehicle
HVT	high-value target
I MEF	1st Marine Expeditionary Force
IA	Iraqi Army
IED	improvised explosive device
IIF	Iraqi Intervention Force
IO	information operations
ISF	Iraqi Security Force
JDAM	Joint Direct Attack Munition
JOC	joint operations center
JRTC	Joint Readiness Training Center
KIA	killed in action
KS	Kansas
LD	line of departure
LOC	line of communication
LSA	logistics support area
LT	lieutenant
LTC	lieutenant colonel
LTG	lieutenant general
MAJ	major
MAM	military-aged male
MCLIC	mine-clearing line charge
MDMP	military decisionmaking process
MEDEVAC	medical evacuation
MG	major general
MGS	mobile gun system
MNC-I	Multinational Corps–Iraq
MNSTC-I	Multinational Security Transition Command–Iraq
MP	military police
MSG	master sergeant
MSR	main supply route
MWD	military working dog
NCO	noncommissioned officer
ODA	Operational Detachment Alpha
OIF	Operation IRAQI FREEDOM
OIF-I	first OIF troop rotation, starting in 2003
OIF-II	second OIF troop rotation, starting in 2004

OIF-III	third OIF troop rotation, starting in 2005
OLE	Operational Leadership Experiences
PFC	private first class
PL	phase line
PSYOP	psychological operations
QRF	quick reaction force
RC	Regional Command
RCT	regimental combat team
recon	reconnaissance
RPG	rocket propelled grenade
S3	Operations Officer
SAPI	Small Arms Protective Insert
SAW	squad automatic weapon
SFC	sergeant first class
SGT	sergeant
SOF	Special Operations Forces
SPC	specialist
SSG	staff sergeant
SUV	Sport Utility Vehicle
TAC	Tactical Command Post
TCP	traffic control point
TF	task force
TOC	tactical operations center
TOW	tube-launched, optically tracked, wire-guided
TPT	tactical psychological operations team
TRADOC	Training and Doctrine Command
TTP	tactics, techniques, and procedures
US	United States
UW	unconventional warfare
VBIED	vehicle-borne improvised explosive device
XO	executive officer

About the Contributors

Pete Boisson retired from the US Army in 2005 and joined the Military History Instructional Support Team of the Combat Studies Institute. Prior to retirement, it was his privilege to serve in Armor Branch with the great Soldiers of the US Army in various assignments around the world. He received a B.A. from the University of San Francisco and a M.P.A. from the Golden Gate University. He resides with his family in Leavenworth, Kansas.

Thomas A. Bruscino, Jr. worked at the US Army Center of Military History in Washington, DC, prior to joining the Combat Studies Institute in December 2005. Dr. Bruscino earned his B.A. in History from Adams State College in Alamosa, Colorado, in 1999, his M.A. in American History from Ohio University in 2002, and his Ph.D. in American Military History from Ohio University in 2005. He is the author of *Out of Bounds: Transnational Sanctuary in Irregular Warfare* (CSI Press, 2006), and his articles and review essays have appeared in the *Claremont Review of Books*, *Journal of America's Military Past*, *San Luis Valley Historian*, and *Reviews in American History.*

Kendall D. Gott retired from the US Army in 2000 having served as an Armor/Cavalry and Military Intelligence officer. A native of Peoria, Illinois, Mr. Gott, received his B.A. in history from Western Illinois University in 1983, and a Masters of Military Art and Science (MMAS) from the US Army Command and General Staff College in 1998. Prior to returning to Kansas in 2002, he was an adjunct professor of history at Augusta State University and the Georgia Military College. Mr. Gott joined the staff of the Combat Studies Institute in October 2002. As Senior Historian of the Research and Publications Team, he conducts historical research and prepares articles and studies on topics of military history.

Ricardo A. Herrera joined the Staff Ride Team, Combat Studies Institute, in January 2006. Before joining CSI, he was director of honors and assistant professor of history at Mount Union College in Alliance, Ohio; previously he was assistant professor of history and department chair at Texas Lutheran University in Seguin, Texas. Dr. Herrera received his Ph.D. in 1998 and M.A. in 1994 from Marquette University and his B.A. from UCLA in 1984. His publications and reviews have appeared in *The Journal of Military History*; *George Washington: Foundation of Leadership and Character* (Praeger, 2001); *1848/1898 @ 1998: Transhistoric Thresholds* (Bilingual Review, Hispanic Research Center, Arizona State University, 2000); *Encyclopedia of War and American Society* (Sage Publications, 2005); *Pennsylvania Magazine of History and Biography*; *Canadian*

Journal of History/Annales canadiennes d'histoire; *Hispanic-American Historical Review*; *Southwestern Historical Quarterly*; and *Maryland Historical Magazine*.

LTC Kevin E. Kennedy, assigned to the Combat Studies Institute since June 2005, serves as a History Instructor and as chief of the Staff Ride Team. Prior to coming to CSI, he served as the battalion S3 and executive officer of the 1st Battalion, 9th Cavalry Regiment for over 2 years, where he participated in Operation IRAQI FREEDOM II. He completed his tour at Fort Hood as the 3d Brigade, 1st Cavalry Division Rear Detachment Commander as the brigade concluded its service in Iraq. LTC Kennedy's civilian education includes a B.A. in History from the University of Arizona and M.A. in Military History from Louisiana State University. His military education includes the Infantry Officer Basic and Advanced Courses, the Combined Arms and Services Staff School, and the Command and General Staff College.

Matt M. Matthews joined the Combat Studies Institute in July 2005 after working for 16 years as a member of the World Class Opposing Force (OPFOR) for the Battle Command Training Program at Fort Leavenworth, Kansas. He graduated from Kansas State University in 1986 with a B.S. in History. Mr. Matthews is the author of *The Posse Comitatus Act and the United States Army: A Historical Perspective* (CSI Press, 2006), *Operation Al FAJR: A Study in Army and Marine Corps Joint Operations* (CSI Press, 2006), and has coauthored numerous scholarly articles on the Civil War.

John J. McGrath worked for 4 years at the US Army Center of Military History in Washington, DC, as a historian and archivist before coming to the Combat Studies Institute in 2002. Mr. McGrath, a graduate of Boston College, holds a M.A. in history from the University of Massachusetts at Boston and is currently a Ph.D. candidate at Kansas State University. He has published several books including *Theater Logistics in the Gulf War* (Army Materiel Command, 1994), *The Brigade: A History* (CSI Press, 2005); *Crossing the Line of Departure* (CSI Press, 2006), and *Boots on the Ground: Troop Density in Contingency Operations* (CSI Press, 2006).